MW00979728

Controversies in Sociology
edited by
Professor T. B. Bottomore and
Professor M. J. Mulkay

20
Cities, Capitalism and Civilization

Controversies in Sociology

Cities, Capitalism and Civilization

R. J. HOLTON

The Flinders University of South Australia

London
ALLEN & UNWIN
Boston   Sydney

Allen & Unwin (Publishers) Ltd,
40 Museum Street, London WC1A 1LU, UK

Allen & Unwin (Publishers) Ltd,
Park Lane, Hemel Hempstead, Herts HP2 4TE, UK

Allen & Unwin, Inc.,
8 Winchester Place, Winchester, Mass. 01890, USA

Allen & Unwin (Australia) Ltd,
8 Napier Street, North Sydney, NSW 2060, Australia

First published in 1986

British Library Cataloguing in Publication Data

Holton, R.J.
    Cities, capitalism and civilization.——
    (Controversies in sociology; 20)
1. Cities and towns——Growth
I. Title   II. Series
307′.14   HT371
ISBN 0–04–301238–8
ISBN 0–04–301217–5 Pbk

Library of Congress Cataloging in Publication Data

Holton, R. J.
    Cities, capitalism, and civilization.
(Controversies in sociology; 20)
Bibliography: p.
Includes index.
1. Sociology, Urban—Methodology.   2. Urbanization.
3. Capitalism—History.   I. Title.   II. Series.
HT151.H634   1986   307.7′6   85–18632
ISBN 0–04–301238–8
ISBN 0–04–301217–5 (pbk.)

Set in 10 on 12 point Times by Phoenix Photosetting, Chatham
and printed in Great Britain by Biddles Ltd, Guildford, Surrey

Contents

Acknowledgements

This book forms part of a larger project on the origins of European capitalism. My decision to work on the specific problem of cities and capitalism owes much to a series of stimulating discussions with Ivan Szelenyi. A preliminary version of the argument in this study was delivered, at his instigation, to the 1982 World Congress of the International Sociological Association in Mexico City. Drafts of further sections were delivered to seminars at the Flinders University of South Australia, the University of Northern Illinois, and the University of Sussex. I am grateful to all who participated in these discussions and to Aidan Southall's generous but critical assistance by correspondence.

I owe a particular debt to Tom Bottomore who encouraged me to tackle the problem of cities and the transition to capitalism in the *Controversies in Sociology* series. I am also grateful to Carol Adams of the University of Sydney for assistance with German translations. Special thanks are also due to Ina Cooper who typed the manuscript with great speed and skill.

1
The city in Western culture

A wide variety of cultures, in many different historical epochs make linguistic distinctions, differentiating the 'central places' of society from that which lies beyond. Modern Western notions of 'city' and 'countryside', with derivations reaching back into the ancient Mediterranean world, form but one instance of a more widespread distinction, evident in cultures as dispersed as Meso-America and China. That the purposes to which such distinctions are put are broadly similar in each of these cases seems highly improbable (Wheatley, 1972). Equally problematic, however, are the specific cultural connotations that have become attached in Western thought to the 'city' and 'countryside'. Foremost among these is the association of the city (or at least some cities) with innovation, social change and modernity. For some this association is interpreted in a positive way, with cities and those who live in them portrayed as agents of 'progress', 'civilization', and 'enlightenment', For others the urban milieu is disapproved of in so far as cities produce social pathology, moral disorder and the destruction of 'community'. Such contrasting prognoses for urban life should not be taken to exclude a third possibility; that in which 'progress' and 'disorder', 'pathology' and 'emancipation', are seen to coexist in the city. Whichever of these views is taken, however, each depends largely on a contrast with the supposed immobility and conservatism of the countryside. This contrast applies whether the rural world is depicted in a benign manner as an Arcadian world of peace and innocence, or is regarded pejoratively as brutish and ignorant.

The intimate relationship between cities and the emergence of Western civilization in its most dynamic and distinctive elements has been rehearsed in the twentieth century in such powerful studies as Lewis Mumford's *The City in History* (1961) and in various works of Gordon Childe concerned with the 'Urban Revolution' beginning in the Middle East (1950, 1960). The aim of the present study is to examine the controversies that have grown up around a particularly striking application of the city/ civilization identification within sociological and historical inquiry. This concerns that set of theories which link the cities of late medieval and early modern Europe with the transition to modern capitalism. This 'urban' dimension to capitalist development represents a prominent thread running through many analyses of the making of the modern Western world. It stretches from the classic work of Adam Smith, Karl Marx, Max Weber and Henri Pirenne (whose various contributions are discussed in Chapter 3 of this study) to more modern work by Fernand Braudel (1973, 1982), Henri Lefebvre (1972, 1976), Antony Giddens (1981) and Gianfranco Poggi (1978, 1983).

In recent years, what might loosely be called the 'urbanist' theory of transition has come under increasing challenge both as to its conceptual coherence and its empirical plausibility. This challenge has developed within five analytically distinct but substantively interrelated types of discourse. These comprise:

1 Discussions oriented towards questions of social, moral and political philosophy. These concern the relationship between the city and the conditions for the realization of human freedom and the 'good society'.
2 Controversies within urban sociology over the possibility of a theoretical specification of the 'urban'.
3 Debates in historical sociology and economic history which consider the role of urban institutions and actors as causal elements in the European transition to capitalism.
4 Studies comparing and contrasting the urban institutions and developmental significance of cities in the European and non-European worlds.
5 Arguments amongst archaeologists, pre-historians, ancient historians and sociologists over the origins of 'civilization' and the place of cities within the civilizing process.

THE CITY IN WESTERN CULTURE

It is important to emphasize that the language of 'city' and 'countryside', 'urban' and 'rural' (and their modern equivalents in most European languages) draws on the powerful and enduring legacy of the ancient Graeco-Roman world within Western thought. This legacy is especially significant in the philosophical underpinnings of urban inquiries, since Graeco-Roman conceptions of 'freedom', 'democracy', 'citizenship' and 'political life' itself are so closely bound up with the ancient city-state, with Rome as the urban centre of the Empire.

The term 'city' in English (*cité* in French, *città* in Italian, *ciudad* in Spanish) derives for example from a set of Latin terms referring to membership of the citizenry (*civitas*) and to the citizen (*civis*). The significance of these institutions in the ancient Roman world arose from classical Greek philosophy where the polity (*polis*) was founded on public citizenship rights. In order to possess such rights of participation in the government of this *polis*, it was necessary to be free, male and a landowner, so as to be able to exercise governing power over the household. It was the possession of these 'household' powers which qualified the holder for the exercise of wider political authority.

It is important to note that the ancient Greeks and Romans did not at the outset identify the condition of citizenship with free propertied city dwellers as such. In the Greek world, as Finley (1977) points out, Aristotle 'took city and hinterland, town and country together as a unit', not as spatially and socially distinct entities. Even those farmers who lived outside the town were integrally part of the *polis*. Although the *polis* was sometimes distinguished from the 'chora', whose meaning approximates to that of rural hinterland (de Ste. Croix, 1981, p. 9), Finley maintains that *polis* served in the main as a term which could be used interchangeably for the 'city-state' or for the 'city'. Later, the Romans took over the Hellenistic practice of regarding the 'city' and its surrounding territory as one unit, that is 'the traditional unity of town and hinterland – political, juridical and residential – went on unchallenged' (Finley, 1977, p. 307). Here the key term *civitas*, was applied to a self-governing community, and would thus apply equally to a group as extensive as the tribes of Gaul as to a 'city'.

None the less, over time citizenship came increasingly to be associated with the public life of the *urbs*, that is, city or town. Urban/rural contrasts were often greatest where cities were settled by migrant groups, both militarily dominant over and culturally distinct from the indigenous population. This occurred in the eastern Hellenistic Mediterranean in places such as Egypt and Asia Minor (Jones, 1937, de Ste Croix, 1981). Even in the less diverse heartlands of ancient Greece and Rome, however, there appeared an increasing contrast between urbanity and rustic life. The urbane qualities pertaining to the *urbanitas* of the city dweller, such as political sophistication, rhetorical excellence or good taste, were contrasted with the 'awkwardness' or ignorance of the country dweller (*choritai*) or rustic (*rusticanus*).

In this manner the political and moral qualities associated with citizenship, such as the capacity for self-government and the right of free men to political participation, became part of a cultural tradition which associated the city as a delimited social and spatial unit with positive values. This clearly contributed to the modern sense of dichotomy between 'urban' and 'rural'. It also remained a constant element in Western thought during the subsequent extension in the meaning of freedom and citizenship from the limited conceptions of political rights practised in slave-based city-states and empires to more universalistic conceptions of citizenship. Thus the formal universalism of the political programme of the French Revolution, for example, was in practice bound up with the city, urban institutions, and the agency of urban rather than landed social classes. The new eighteenth century term 'civilization' (Elias, 1978) itself carried strongly urban, as distinct from rural, connotations. The 'good life' it seems depended on the political victory of city over countryside.

However strong the linguistic and political legacy of the classical world may be, modern urban/rural dichotomies and the connection between urbanity, progress, civilization and the development of capitalism are not derived in any straightforward way from the ancient Mediterranean. In the first place, as we have seen, the political structure of the city-state based on land-owning citizens ruled out any clear-cut distinction between urban dwellers and rural dwellers. The city-state was then an organization of land holders not as yet exclusively dependent on urban property or on an exclusively urban way of life. One indication of this is the development of the villa as both the economic base and rural seat of the urban patricians of the Roman world. While the villa system may be evidence of the 'Romanization' of the countryside, it cannot easily be translated into 'modern' spatial and cultural distinctions between city and countryside as thoroughly discrete entities. This is reflected linguistically within the Roman world in the practice of classifying the residential buildings of a country estate as the *villa* (or *pars*) *urbana*, distinct from those devoted to the support of economic life, referred to as the *villa* (or *pars*) *rustica* (Leveau, 1983). This indicates a sense of differentiation between 'urban' and 'rustic', but not one that is coterminous either with modern spatial distinctions between urban and rural, or with functional distinctions between progressive urban and backward landed economies.

A second intimately related problem with any simplistic attempt to derive modern categories from those of the classical world is the indifference towards explicitly 'economic' relations as these are now understood within ancient conceptions of 'urban' and 'rural'. While the early Greek citizen bodies were made up to a significant extent of working farmers (Anderson, 1974a, pp. 29–33), over time the notion of free citizenship came to be associated with exclusion from direct manual labour. The ideal of the citizen referred to a primarily political and juridical classification, rather than discrimination between different classes of economic actors. The fusion of notions like citizenship and political freedom with the economic dimensions of urban activity (such as trade and industry) is a much later historical phenomenon.

While emphasizing the Graeco-Roman influence on subsequent Western urban-centred conceptions of civilization, it is important to avoid the trap of assuming that all aspects of the ancient world led directly towards more modern occidental conceptions of urbanism. In the first place, the self-governing *polis* of the Hellenistic world had, by the later Roman Empire, been subsumed within and to an extent destroyed by the primarily Imperial modes of political authority. The imperial ideal was of course revived in the establishment of the Holy Roman Empire.

However, this institution was never sufficiently effective to undermine the revival of autonomous cities in the medieval period. In addition, the centralized imperial control over cities that remained in the eastern Roman or Byzantine Empire after the fall of Rome tended not towards the 'Western' *polis* pattern of urban autonomy developing within medieval Europe, but to an alternative pattern in which cities did not emerge as autonomous entities *per se*. This was evident both in the Byzantine Empire, and from the seventh century onwards in the Islamic cities of the Middle East and North Africa. The Graeco-Roman legacy is therefore neither unitary nor exclusively confined to the history of the West (von Grunebaum, 1970).

Two further historical influences underlie the 'urbanist' character of much modern Western social and political philosophy. The first involves the notion of 'city' as a refuge or haven from inhospitable coercive and immoral influences outside. Within Western thought this theme draws in large measure on St Augustine's celebrated study *The City of God* (*civitas dei*). Written in the early fifth century after the sacking of Rome by the Goths, St Augustine counterpoised the divine City of God with the immorality and decadence of the earthly city. The sack of Rome, he said, should not upset the Christian faith, since Christians (or at least the Christian elect) have a sanctuary in the 'pilgrim city of God'. Such ideas of urban sanctuary from sin and immorality and urban support for salvation were not, however, exclusively other-worldly. Both cities – the heavenly and the earthly – are in a metaphorical sense present in this world within two distinct 'communities' of the godly and ungodly, but in the next life only the Elect will dwell in the City of God.

St Augustine's eschatology has been seen as relatively conventional in terms of the traditions of Judao-Christianity. His connection between city, refuge and salvation, however metaphorical at the outset, was later to become of considerable significance in medieval Europe. The notion of the City of God as sanctuary, for example, had considerable influence as a legitimation for the challenge of urban ecclesiastical jurisdictions to the secular powers of princes and the landed nobility. This was often linked to the idea of a New Jerusalem representing some future Kingdom of Heaven on Earth. In the extreme case of

Florence in the epoch of Savonarola this found expression in a new urban millenarianism (Burke, 1972, p. 186). But in a more diffuse sense the utopian, eschatalogical elements in writings such as St Augustine's helped to inject into Western Christianity and Western thought more generally the idea of a connection between cities, human emancipation from worldly conflict, and participation in the creation of a new order. Such elements were to continue in a potent way with the 'utopian' elements in classical political philosophy. Much twentieth-century urban planning may be interpreted as a secularization of this utopian and visionary thread in Western thought.

A further set of historical influences on the language and political philosophy of the Western city derives from the Germanic world of northern Europe. Here the proverb 'town air makes free' (*Stadtluft macht frei*) has become enshrined as a symbol of the historic association of late medieval and early modern European cities with freedom and liberation from oppression. The precise origins of this sentiment within Germanic history are not altogether clear. Linguistically, the Germanic languages have certainly contributed to the stock of modern terms within which the emancipatory claims of urban life have been conducted. Foremost among these are the words 'burg', 'burgh', or 'borough', deriving from Old Teutonic, Saxon and Norse, meaning fortress or place of shelter. It is from these roots that terms like 'burgher', 'bourgeois' and 'bourgeoisie' – the ostensible urban agents of capitalist expansion – derive. Similarly, the term 'town' has a Germanic derivation, referring to a walled place.

It is doubtful, however, that the German tribes knew 'urban' life of a kind similar to that which had developed in the classical world. Such terms as 'burg' or 'town' appear to have derived originally from names for large areas enclosed by fortifications to serve as places of refuge during war and possibly semi-permanent residences for pastoralists – the equivalent of the Roman *oppida*. These fortified places did not constitute cities on the 'model' of the classical world (Musset, 1975). The subsequent contact and merging of the Germanic tribes with what remained of the classical urbanist legacy after the decline of Rome led at a later date however to a linguistic fusion of

Germanic and Roman terms to produce words like the Germanic–Latin *burgarius* and the middle Latin *burgensis* (Riedel, 1975) referring to town dwellers.

While the German language retained the term *bürger* for townsmen, rather than adopting words derived from the Latin *civatas* and *civis*, the bulk of late medieval political and juridical conceptions of urban citizenship derived either from classical authors like Aristotle, or from Christian notions of citizenship in God (*Gottesburgerschaft*) as presented by St Augustine. In this manner, a Western sense of the city as both a protected (i.e. walled) social milieu and as a context for a freer exchange of goods and ideas for social improvement, became consolidated. The resulting notion of the city has been symbolized by Robert Lopez (1963) as 'the cross' or 'crossroads' within the 'walls'. This metaphor suggests a combination of protected social space and intercommunication between those coming from different directions to the crossroads of urban life. To this may be added a further metaphorical sense of religious legitimation for urban projects, through the idea of the protecting 'cross'.

Such long-run historical developments within the classical Christian and Germanic worlds form much of the linguistic, cultural and philosophical context of more modern associations between the city, progress and freedom. They undoubtedly became consolidated in late medieval and early modern Europe, both with the expansion of urban settlements and the emergence of legitimate 'urban' jurisdictions over matters of legal process, economic policy and social welfare. The much emphasized development of 'urban' communes of propertied men capable of bearing arms, during the eleventh and twelfth centuries, drew on Graeco-Roman conceptions of free citizenship, Christian notions of the city as refuge, and on Germanic ideas of the town as fortress. By the fourteenth and fifteenth centuries, the pictorial depiction of the cities of Renaissance Italy, France or the Low Countries, whose extensive street plans are contained by city walls, gives a striking evocation of the self-consciousness of the city dweller at this moment in European history.

What is far more problematic with respect to the central theme of this book is how far European city dwellers at this time saw the city and urbanity in economic rather than juridical, political and religious terms. The ideational content of urban self-consciousness is not, of course, decisive to the question of how far the transition to capitalism depended on urban sources of enterprise and innovation. The emergence of capitalism may after all have been an unintended consequence of social action devoted to quite other ends. Within late medieval European culture, it appears that the burghers and burgesses were more likely to be closely involved in economic activity (associated very often with guilds) than the Roman citizenry. At the same time the cultural meaning of terms like 'burgher' and its various equivalents remained embedded in types of discourse concerned primarily with political authority, jurisdictional competence and social status.

The German school of *Begriffsgeschichte* (conceptual history) has warned against 'the careless transfer of modern context-determined expressions . . . to the past' (Koselleck, 1982, pp. 415–16). It has also been pointed out that 'words such as "bürger" which have remained in constant use are in themselves no sufficient indication of stability of substantial meaning' (ibid.). In Chapter 4 it will be argued that the apparent historical continuity in the evolution of terms from 'burgess/burgher' to 'bourgeoisie' conceals an important discontinuity between a late medieval politico-juridical notion and modern economic conceptions of class tied to capitalist property relations. The attribution of the latter to the former therefore amounts to a misleading anachronistic imputation.

The unequivocal view of cities and the Western bourgeoisie as centres of *economic progress* as well as political virtue and social emancipation from tyranny is then very much a product of the nineteenth century industrial capitalist transformation of Europe. This extension of the 'urban' ideal is clearly tied up with the emergence of a sense of economic life as a self-subsistent and dominant force in the shaping of human society. It is important to stress that such understandings were neither age-old nor simple extensions of the world-views of the Graeco-Roman or medieval Christian worlds. They depended rather on the powerful effect of a set of technological and organizational changes which by the early nineteenth century had demonstrated the remarkable new capacity for humankind to exploit the natural environment to meet social ends. It is customary to refer to the concentrated impact of such changes as the 'Industrial Revolution', though the sharp discontinuity with the past that this term suggests is somewhat misleading if it implies a static Europe prior to this epoch.

One of the most striking concomitants of such increases in human productive capacity was the development of a sense of 'society' and the social realm of human labour and artifice as distinct from that of 'nature'. At the same time the 'industrial' and primarily urban location of the new economic dynamism after 1750 served to emphasize the connection between 'society' and the 'city', while the 'countryside' (*le paysage*) and its inhabitants (*les paysans*) were equated with the realm of 'nature' or as Marx put it 'rural idiocy'.

Such pejorative constructions of the 'countryside' have some affinity with the ancient Roman distinction between 'urban' and 'rural' whereby the 'urbane' city dwellers looked down with sophisticated disdain on the 'rustic'. Distinctions of this kind were of course primarily political and juridical, with boundaries being drawn between free and unfree social actors. Such connotations have certainly persisted in European thought in the use made of terms like 'urbane' and 'rustic'. Nevertheless, the historic abandonment of slavery, and the emergence of the peasantry as a subordinate 'estate' alongside the 'nobility' and the 'clerics', now integrated those who lived by manual labour with the corporate structure of society. It should not then be too surprising to find the term 'rustic' being used by thirteenth century peasant shepherds in the French Pyrenees as a term of abuse for their neighbours (Le Roy Ladurie, 1978a, p. 57). The irony of this situation, by both classical and nineteenth century standards, is a not insignificant reminder that notions of the countryside as 'natural' repositories of innocence or idiocy are cultural constructions; constructions, it might be added, which have been highly pertinent to the legitimation of modern urban claims to political authority and economic exploitation of the countryside.

Rather than a straightforward derivation from the classical world, the pejorative view of the countryside and rural 'economic' backwardness is in large measure the product of a modern, largely nineteenth century, triumphalist urban ideology. Raymond Williams (1975), for example, has shown for the

English case that use of city/countryside distinctions to differentiate the 'urbane' and 'progressive' from the 'rustic' and 'backward' emerged comparatively slowly between the sixteenth and
eighteenth centuries, acquiring 'modern' connotations by the
nineteenth century. In this instance, it may be hypothesized that
the problematic and historically contingent character of these
taken-for-granted terms relate to changes in the economic structure of 'city' and 'countryside'. As will be outlined in more detail
in Chapter 4, the rural industries and agrarian expansion of early
modern Europe were only really overtaken or checked at an
aggregate level by urban-industrial dynamism during the late
eighteenth and early nineteenth centuries. While there are many
examples of dynamic cities from Venice and Bruges to
Amsterdam and London prior to this time, it was not until the
mid to late eighteenth century that the relative weight of the
urban-industrial sector became sufficient to bring about rural
de-industrialization and the 'bourgeoisification' of agrarian landowners. There is therefore a strong possibility – and one which
underlies the entire structure of this study – that the conventional
dichotomy between dynamic capitalist cities and the conservative feudalistic countryside is an *ex post facto* folk myth of the
modern Western bourgeoisie and its urbanist intellectuals. The
familiar 'Whig theory of history' in which a civilized urban patriciate or middle class is somehow always on the 'rise' and at the
centre of cumulative social progress is one powerful repository of
this idea.

From the eighteenth century onwards, Western liberal and
socialist political philosophy has in general been strongly pro-
urban. Legitimized in part by their historical derivation in the
classical and Christian past of Western civilization, the actions of
urban social classes and interest groups have been at the centre of
two interrelated movements effectively promoting the dominance of city over countryside. In the first place, urban liberal
and socialist movements challenged the political power and
social status of traditional landed classes. The aim was to shift the
basis of government away from arbitrary, autocratic or despotic
power towards the rule of law and universal citizenship rights.
This involved the dismantling of absolutism and venality of
office, the extension of the franchise, and the opening of public

office to appointment by merit rather than status. None the less, while the logic of universalistic theory was to undermine 'urban' and 'rural' distinctions in the name of equal citizenship, for the moment urban political radicalism was in general sceptical if not hostile to the possibility that the countryside might be a repository of 'progressive' political forces. Not without some reason did rural voters – actual or potential – tend to be regarded as clients or dupes of conservative landed interest.

Secondly, urban groups challenged many of the economic institutions and much of the economic power of landed groups. This was reflected in policies to open up the countryside in a less regulated manner than hitherto to market forces. Liberal opinion in particular sought to challenge rural monopolies and protective devices such as the English Corn Laws designed to keep up rural profits and rent receipts, if necessary at the expense of cheap bread. With the exception of certain currents of anarchism and anti-urban Romanticism, most sections of liberal and socialist opinion in the nineteenth century saw progress in terms of the economic and political victory of the city over the countryside. This viewpoint obtained, in spite of awareness of social ills such as poverty, disease, pollution and crime, that were increasingly perceived in the urban context. Such conditions may have brought about a certain ambivalence towards actual nineteenth century cities, but they did not as yet undermine the ideal of the city, if reformed or liberated from oppressive relations, as the locus of social development.

In the case of Marx and Engels, for example, the deplorable social conditions of the mid-Victorian city were problems of capitalist urbanization, rather than of the city itself (Engels, 1969). Such problems, together with the continuing 'idiocy' or 'barbarism' of the rural populations of Europe and the world beyond, could be tackled by a combination of the further internationalization of European capitalist urbanization, and the transcendence of capitalist urban forms by socialism. Marx, like the liberal urban scholars of Pirenne and Weber some sixty years later, did not doubt that the city formed the crucible for the dynamic economic and political development of occidental history.

The pro-urban ideologies of nineteenth century European

liberalism and socialism were a constituent part of the first generation of sociological analysis of urban/rural distinctions. As such they provide the standards of cultural relevance that underlie the origins of the other 'urban' discourses in urban sociology, comparative historical sociology and economic and social history. Throughout this period, various conservative, Romantic or populist critiques of urban civilization have, of course, been offered as alternative philosophies of human freedom and social order. It was not until the twentieth century, however, and more especially in the post-war period, that 'anti-urban' critiques began to make much headway within the mainstream of Western social and historical theory. The intensity of this recent challenge, which represents far more than a renewal of the conservative or Romantic position, is associated with a number of important economic trends and political processes evident in the twentieth century.

The specificity of the urban milieu in the contemporary world has proved increasingly elusive under the impact of processes of national and international centralization associated with the nation-state and the international capitalist economy or world system. Where cities and urban actors have become subsumed in wider processes such as these, it is not easy to regard urban institutions and actors as discrete structures on which to rest hopes for social change. Within this contemporary context at least, it seems inappropriate to invoke the historical claim that 'urban air makes free', since the context of social and political action is primarily national and international.

This subsumption of the 'urban' is reinforced by the contemporary blurring of historically derived distinctions between 'city' and 'countryside'. With the continuing decline of 'rural' peasant societies in the West, and the penetration of the countryside by phenomena conventionally associated with 'urbanism', such as the relocation of large-scale enterprises, and the development of commuter centres, it becomes increasingly difficult to insist on urban/rural distinctions as indicating progressive or conservative social spaces.

Finally, the twentieth century has seen a significant number of successful peasant-based revolutionary movements within the Third World against Western colonialism and imperialism. This has prompted some metropolitan socialists to the view that the achievement of socialism does not necessarily mean either 'the political victory of urban dwellers over rural dwellers' (as has conventionally been assumed in Western transitions to capitalism and socialism), or the victory of urban proletarians over rural peasants (as in Soviet models of transition to socialism and communism). One possible implication of this is that it is not only urban air that can make free. An alternative possibility, canvassed by Wallerstein (1984), is that socialism requires not so much the maximization of free urban air, as the transcendence of the urban/rural distinction. Instead of relying on Western liberalism for its conception of the free city of economic producers, socialism should be thought of as 'the city-state writ large' (ibid., p. 71). For Wallerstein, mindful of the political philosophy of Aristotle, the city-state connotes an entity wider than the idealized 'urban' polities of nineteenth century thought.

The faltering of various urbanist philosophies of social change in the contemporary Western setting has not led to a wholesale abandonment of the notions of urban institutions or urbanity as discrete phenomena. Even such a powerful critic of urbanist ideology as Castells (1977) retains a delimited conception of the functional importance of the city as the sphere for collective consumption, as opposed to economic production, and as the locale for radical urban social movements mobilized over collective consumption issues within the capitalist mode of production. Three significant types of responses have none the less appeared as a result of the challenge to produce a tighter specification of the urban. The first, and least satisfactory from the viewpoint of cross-cultural research, is the subjectivist option that a town is present when people feel it to be (Jones, 1966, Beaujeu-Garnier and Chabod, 1967). This does little more than beg the question as to the criteria by which we recognize some shared substantive content to various expressions of this kind. The second response is to abandon or suspend the search for a general trans-contextual theory of urbanity in favour of a plurality of particular types of 'city'. This approach, deriving from the work of Weber (1968), has the paradoxical effect of grouping together different types of 'city' without being very clear about what it is that all variants have in common (see also Hoselitz,

1953, Braudel, 1973). The third response is to regard urban/rural distinctions as more appropriate to the historical context of western European transition to capitalism, than to the contemporary world. This had produced a line of argument which conceives of the 'urban' as a historical rather than sociological object of inquiry (Saunders, 1981). The dubious logical coherence of displacing the 'urban' from a sociological to an historical object of inquiry will be examined in more detail in Chapter 2 in the context of a critical review of the concepts of city and urban life.

It is doubtful whether any major analyst of the emergence of Western capitalism, prior to 1945, could have conceived of this process without attributing a leading, if not decisive, role to institutions and actors located in cities. Such notions as 'transition to capitalism', 'Industrial Revolution', and 'Rationalization', encompass many themes. These include technological change and the factory system, the growth of world markets, changes in property rights and in the structure of legitimate domination, and the emergence of 'rational' liberal democratic states. Such themes have none the less been seen as intimately connected with cities. These are taken both as centres of innovation and as the domain of the middle class or bourgeoisie. Two further issues, however, are less clear-cut. In the first place it is not clear how much weight analysts like Marx, Weber and Pirenne wished to place on 'urban' as opposed to 'extra-urban' changes in the emergence of capitalism. Secondly, and even more crucially, there is the difficulty of determining whether the intention was to portray the city and urban institutions as autonomous causal forces in their own right, rather than expressions of some more fundamental influence.

Chapter 3 will be devoted to a re-examination of the work of the 'classical' urbanist theorists. Particular attention will be given to demonstration of the problematic causal status of such key concepts as 'city', 'countryside', '*Bürgertum*' and 'bourgeoisie'. This group of theorists do not emerge as quite so unambiguously committed to an urbanist theory of transition as is sometimes thought.

It was not until the post-war period that explicit controversy over the role of cities in the transition to capitalism fully emerged. One of the main stimuli behind it was the publication

of Maurice Dobb's *Studies in The Development of Capitalism* in
1947. The ensuing debate between Dobb, Sweezy and many
others ranged over a number of themes within the Marxist developmental paradigm of transition from the feudal to the capitalist
modes of production. (For a critical review of these debates see
Holton (1981) and (1985).) Dobb, while influenced by the earlier
work of Marx and Pirenne, presented a powerful critique of the
proposition that the urban institutions and burghers of late
feudal Europe could be regarded as decisive elements in this
transition. Dobb's alternative drew rather on Marx's discussion
of the agrarian basis of transition involving such processes as the
dispossession of the peasantry, the differentiation of petty
commodity producers between capitalists and wage-labourers,
the concentration of landed property in private hands and the
class struggle over private property rights. The 'free' cities of the
late medieval world were seen as an intrinsic part of the 'feudal
world' rather than independent centres of decisive importance to
the process of capitalist development.

The intellectual impact and plausibility of this line of argument, developed in more recent work by Hilton (1969, 1973,
1978) and Brenner (1976, 1977, 1982), will be examined in
Chapter 4 in the context of a broader survey of sociological and
historical literature. Two further major points of debate will also
be introduced. The first involves the emergence of neo-
Malthusian arguments concerning population and food supply as
important elements of the agrarian and rural industrial context of
capitalist development. This work has tended to reinforce the
arguments of those who emphasize agrarian rather than urban
preconditions for successful capitalist development. The second
area of discussion concerns the highly problematic relationship
between cities and the development of nation-states. One of the
major problems faced both by Marxists and urbanist theorists of
transition is why Western capitalism should have developed
within a national rather than urban political framework. Chapter
4 also draws upon a diverse range of monographic work by
historians of medieval and modern Europe in order to assess the
empirical plausibility of the various theoretical objections to the
urbanist case. Within this overall process of critique attention
will also be given to certain recent reformulations of the urbanist

position, notably by Merrington (1975) and Poggi (1983). These are important in so far as they offer a more balanced appreciation of the strengths and weaknesses of conventional statements of the urbanist explanation of transition.

A further preoccupation of the 'classical' theorists of European urbanization and the transition to capitalism was the comparison between Western and non-Western (for example, 'Asiatic') cities. The contrast between the dynamic Western pathway of social change and the conservatism or restricted basis of non-Western urban development is a prominent theme in the work of both Marx and Weber. Such important theoretical statements reflect the significant element of comparative discourse built from the outset into debates about cities and capitalism founded on the premise of the 'uniqueness' of the West. With the expansion of comparative urban history and sociology since 1945, this area of inquiry can now be usefully regarded as a discourse in its own right. The underlying premise of this comparative approach is that an evaluation of urbanist theories of the emergence of Western capitalism cannot be based simply on an internal history of Europe. Chapter 5 presents a survey of recent research into the characteristics and developmental consequences of 'cities' for processes of social change. On the basis of literature dealing with Islamic, Chinese, Russian and east European cities an attempt is made both to establish how far the Western city was 'unique' and to ascertain the developmental significance of urban contrasts. This discussion is linked back to the problem of the inadequacy of generic definitions of the city, on which urban contrasts might be founded, raised in Chapter 2. An attempt is made to resolve such difficulties by arguing that ostensible 'urban' contrasts may more properly be seen in part in terms of variations in the structure of political authority.

A final discourse, whose bearing on the Western transition process is less widely appreciated, concerns pre-history and the history of the ancient world. It is here that one may find certain contemporary statements of the proposition that cities over the last six to ten millennia have been synonymous with 'civilization' and the 'civilizing process'. While the classically trained analysts of the nineteenth and early twentieth centuries were steeped in the legacy of the ancient Mediterranean world in the making of the modern West, this long-run perspective had until very recently receded in importance within the mainstream of contemporary sociology and history. Some recent work by Jane Jacobs (1970) Anderson (1974a) and Giddens (1981) has now sought to restore this longer time-frame to the analysis of cities and social change. Amongst other benefits, this has served to liberate historical sociology from a predominantly foreshortened chronology concentrated on the transition from the medieval or feudal to the modern or capitalist worlds.

In the concluding chapter, an attempt is made to establish the importance of this wider time-frame to the understanding of both the coherence and plausibility of urbanist theories connecting capitalism and the development of Western civilization. Particular attention is given to the doubts that have arisen over the possibility that the historic relationship between Western cities and the rise of capitalism represents one example of a more universal connection between cities and progress going back to ancient times. The use of ancient reference points in the historical sociology of Western cities is none the less illuminating in so far as it throws light on some alternative ways of conceiving of the place of city and countryside within the development of human society in general and Western society in particular.

2
The city in social theory: some problems

The 'city' appears as such a prominent feature of social life in so many contrasting cultures and historical epochs that one might suppose the question of what all such 'cities' have in common to be long-settled. Yet this supposition is quite unwarranted. However impressive the monumental public buildings, the spatially concentrated specialist urban functions, and the self-conscious pride of city dwellers may seem from time to time, the attempt to provide a generic conceptualization of the city has proved an elusive, and some would say fruitless, quest for urban sociologists and historians. While many scholars operate as if terms like 'city' and 'countryside', 'urban' and 'rural' were grounded in unproblematic definitions, grave doubts have been raised as to the coherence of the idea of the city and of urban social institutions as discrete objects of social analysis and as autonomous causal forces in their own right.

The logical status of the city within social theory was left obscure by nineteenth- and early twentieth-century thinkers, a state of affairs which has not been successfully resolved in more recent work. It has often been emphasized that Marx, Weber and Durkheim did not propose that the city should be seen as a social reality *sui generis*, distinct from surrounding patterns of social relations. What was required was not an explicit theory of the city as a generic social structure, but rather an awareness that cities were coterminous with some more fundamental set of social relations, whether private property relations (Marx), structures of legitimate domination (Weber) or the division of labour (Durkheim). And yet the matter is more complex than this. Abrams (1978), for example, has demonstrated that Marx and Weber were at times so struck by the apparent discreteness and autonomy of cities at certain stages in world history as to be tempted to treat the city itself as a major causal factor in the process of social change. They were impressed in particular with the late medieval and early modern period in European history where they interpreted the emergence of urban communes and the differentiation of the bourgeoisie from traditional social structures as evidence of the causal significance of urban institutions for processes of social change. The activity of cities and urban social classes was conceived, moreover, in sharp contrast to the conservatism of the countryside.

Marx certainly wavered between treating the city as an autonomous generic structure to be found in all societies characterized by private property and the division of labour, and viewing it as a heterogenous institution whose form varied according to the property relations of different modes of production. The former interpretation is clearly represented in *The German Ideology*. Here Marx and Engels claim that:

> The most important division of material and mental labour is the separation of town and country. The contradiction between town and country begins with the transition from barbarism to civilisation, from tribe to state, from locality to nation, and runs through the whole history of civilisation to the present day . . . The town is in actual fact already the concentration of the population, of the instruments of production, of capital, of pleasures, of needs, while the country demonstrates just the opposite fact, isolation and separation. (Marx and Engels, 1976, p. 72)

In *Pre-capitalist Formations*, written a dozen or so years later, Marx demonstrates a far greater awareness of the heterogenous character of city/countryside relations. Here urban forms are seen as dependent on the over-arching structure of the mode of production. In the context of a more sophisticated discussion of the historic emergence of private property, Marx formulates the heterogeneous place of the city in world history as follows:

> The Germanic community is not concentrated in the city, a concentration . . . which gives the community as such an

external existence distinct from that of its individual members. Ancient classical history is the history of cities, but cities based on landownership and agriculture; Asian history is a kind of undifferentiated unity of town and country (the large city, properly speaking, must be regarded merely as a princely camp, superimposed on the real economic structure); the Middle Ages (Germanic period) starts with the countryside as the locus of history, whose further development then proceeds through the opposition of town and country; modern (history) is the urbanisation of the countryside, not as among the ancients, the ruralisation of the city. (Marx, 1965b, pp. 77–8)

While Szelenyi (1981) regards this as the most 'concise and provocative formulation of the urban question for the purpose of a historically and comparatively grounded sociology', Merrington (1975) is probably right to be more sanguine as to its utility. He sees Marx's comments as a 'Sybilline indication' (ibid., p. 77) pointing the way to issues that require analysis, such as the relative weight of 'urban' and 'rural' elements within particular phases of social change, rather than supplying any clear-cut hypotheses as to the role of the city and countryside at various stages in world history.

As far as the specific problem of the transition from feudalism to capitalism is concerned there is certainly a suggestion of urban/rural opposition founded on urban initiatives, that is, the urbanization of the countryside, as a key to the emergence of capitalism. Yet there is also great uncertainty as to whether Marx has regarded the 'city' in this process of opposition as a fundamentally discontinuous entity compared with what went before the Germanic period, or whether he has retained an implicit sense of the city as a generic unity. This latter possibility is implied in the use of such notions as 'city in antiquity', 'the medieval opposition of town and country', and so on. We lack, however, any clear sense of the common quality that allows us to speak of various entities as 'cities' or 'countrysides'. This, as Abrams demonstrates, follows from Marx and Engels' wish to subsume the city and urban institutions – including the so-called 'urban' problems of nineteenth century cities – beneath a more generic structure based on comparisons between different forms of property rights over the product of labour. Marx's wavering from this view in favour of a generic sense of city is to be explained by the fact that the city 'is a social form in which the essential properties or larger systems of social relations are grossly concentrated and intensified to a point where . . . the formal characteristics of the town appear to be in themselves constituent properties of a distinct social order' (Abrams, 1978, pp. 9–10).

Max Weber developed his views on cities and social change on a far more elaborate historical and comparative canvas than did Marx. Yet here again we find a definite ambivalence towards the problem of whether cities can be treated as generic social entities. In the first section of Weber's work on the city, published in *Economy and Society* (1968), an underlying quest for generic definition of the city is evident. Having rehearsed a range of possibilities, including demographic size and concentration, economic function as a market centre and political-administrative function as a 'fortress' and centre of authority Weber is drawn increasingly away from this initial quest. What is emphasized instead is the sheer heterogeneity of urban forms across time and space. Thus there are 'merchant' and 'producer' cities defined by economic function, but also 'consumer' and 'rentier' cities parasitic on producers elsewhere, together with 'fortress' 'garrison' and 'administrative' cities whose connection with economic life is not necessarily very significant. Of course many of these functions may be combined in the one location. Even so, no generic property which all cities share is identified. Heterogeneity appears to dominate over homogeneity.

While Weber is certainly not immune from the temptation to seek a generic basis to the role of the city in world history, a far stronger theme in his work is the assimilation of urban/feudal distinctions to a far clearer generic discussion of the types of legitimate domination. The ostensibly urbanist discourse in *Economy and Society* (republished by Martindale under the title of *The City*) is not strictly speaking urban sociology. Weber's own title takes the city, and more especially the cities of late medieval and early modern Europe, as instances of non-legitimate domination. Weber's claim is that certain traditional relations of domination were 'usurped' by new urban social agents whose newly established political and juridical institutions presaged the rational-legal domination of the modern 'period'. The ambivalence in Weber, as in Marx, is to be found in the vacillation between the wish to produce a comparative historical sociology of cities and social change – which must logically require a generic conception of the city as an organizing premise – and the even stronger theoretical perception that cities in the final analysis are not autonomous causal entities but elements in a wider social structure. What both contributions lack is an explicit recognition of the likelihood that definition of the 'city' is impossible in principle, since what are referred to as urban institutions and classes have no autonomous reality *sui generis*.

Durkheim's comments on the city as the locus of an extensive division of labour and of the transition to modern forms of social structure are less elaborate than those of Marx or Weber, and have made little impact on recent analyses by historians of the specific problem of the transition to capitalism. While there is no real attempt in Durkheim to produce a generic notion of the city, his view of great cities as 'the uncontested homes of progress' (1933, p. 296) reflects the urban-centred view of social change that he shared with Marx and Weber. Where Durkheim has been more influential is in his account of transition to the modern city as the locus for shifts from mechanical to organic solidarity. Here his explicit intention is to show that undifferentiated forms of traditional social solidarity are eroded in the course of urbanization with the development of individuation and social diversity based on the division of labour. This process is not unproblematic, however, since 'transition' could under certain circumstances provoke anomie and social breakdown in the form of crime and suicide.

In so far as Durkheim subsumed the city under the broader analysis of social solidarity he left no explicit warrant for attempts to produce a generic conception of the city as an autonomous causal force. His picture of the city in transition, combining the release of economic and moral individualism from previous constraints together with the growth of incipient problems of social pathology, none the less fed into twentieth-century scholarship. Here, especially within urban sociology, the quest for a generic definition of the city was resumed.

While Durkheim and Marx saw modern society as increasingly obliterating distinctions between city and countryside through the progressive 'urbanization' of society itself, Georg Simmel and Louis Wirth (himself heavily influenced by Simmel's student, Robert Park) chose to maintain an emphasis on the distinctive character of 'urban' social life as such. The focus here is in a sense not urban as such but metropolitan, reflecting Simmel's background in Berlin (Frisby, 1981, pp. 11–12, 19). For Simmel and Wirth it was the distinctive and autonomous cultural features of the metropolis which encouraged them to reassert urban distinctiveness. In Simmel's case a combination of the scale of large cities and their constitution through an extended division of labour produced 'a deep contrast with small town and rural life' (Simmel quoted in Wolff, 1950, p. 420). In the metropolis, direct interaction between persons known to each other gave way to a greater impersonality, producing enlarged individual freedom, a stronger sense of individual self, and a more powerful calculative element in social life.

While it is arguable that Simmel's sociology of number comes close to providing a theory of the city *per se*, there remains some doubt as to whether the emphasis on metropolis is sufficiently all-embracing to count as a generic account of urbanity itself. The metropolis appears more as an index of rationalization. In Wirth's work on urbanism, by contrast, an explicit definition of the city, at least in ideal-typical form, is erected on the basis of a range of clear-cut empirical criteria. This features 'a relatively large, dense and permanent settlement of socially heterogenous individuals' involving a way of life founded on values such as individualism (Wirth, 1938, p. 8). In this way Wirth sought to rectify what he took to be a defect in the existing rich literature of the city, where 'we look in vain for a theory systematising the available knowledge concerning the city as a social entity' (ibid., p. 4).

The twentieth-century emergence of a stronger generic sense of the city, in comparison with the more muted and ambivalent discussions of Marx, Weber and Durkheim, has been consolidated in attempts by sociologists of development to treat urbanity and urbanization as autonomous causal agents in social change (Lerner, 1958, Reissman, 1964). Such procedures rely on the reaffirmation of urban/rural differences. In urban sociology and urban history since 1945, the notion of the city as both an autonomous social force with a universal generic set of characteristics and a progressive force in stimulating social change was widespread. It may be found in Sjoberg's important study on *The Pre-Industrial City* (1960) where 'certain structural elements' connected with organization of power are taken as 'universal for all urban centres'. Braudel's magisterial studies – *Capitalism and Material Life* (1973) and *The Wheels of Commerce* (1982) – involves the presupposition that 'all towns have certain common characteristics and such characteristics more or less persist from one period to another'.

A further striking stimulus to generic theorizing about the city has come from central-place theory which emerged in the first instance within human geography (Christaller, 1933). Here cities are presented as at the apex of a hierarchy of spatial locations, in which special functions (usually economic) are performed that are unavailable elsewhere. The credentials of this theory as a generic account of cities have come under criticism in so far as they depend on assumptions of market exchange. Giddens (1981, p.144), while alert to such problems, has none the less retained the geopolitical metaphor of 'central-place' as a way of reconstituting a generic view of the city as a 'storage container' for power.

Like many theorists before him, Giddens has remained ambivalent as to what conceptual status to give to the city. On the assumption that there are three logical alternatives to defining the city, namely:

1 As a generic universalistic and autonomous institution.
2 As a non-universal historically contingent but still autonomous institution.
3 As a non-autonomous institution subsumed within some more fundamental pattern of social relations.

Giddens, in his discussion in *A Contemporary Critique of Historical Materialism*, manages to hold to all three positions simultaneously.

During the 1950s and 1960s there also emerged a spate of

literature criticizing the belief that terms like 'urban' and 'rural' could be linked with any consistent contrasts in social organization, economic function or set of cultural values. Such criticisms were based in part on empirical findings drawn from both European and Third World settings. These showed, amongst other things, that urban/rural dichotomies failed to recognize the coexistence of supposedly urban and rural characteristics in a range of settings, and that they failed to take sufficient account of the vast diversity of social arrangements that exist in association with ostensibly urban forms (Foster, 1953, Stewart, 1958, Hauser, 1965).

This line of criticism is not necessarily damaging to notions of 'urban' and 'rural' as ideal-types designed to clarify discrete logical possibilities in the definition of social institutions. Wirth's conception of urbanism as a way of life is not, for example, rebutted simply by the empirical presence of certain communitarian or close personal links within the city. A more defensible response to the critique of urban/rural dichotomies has been to think of urban/rural as poles on a complex continuum. This procedure, however, has itself come under empirical challenge. Pahl (1968), for example, has argued that there is little empirical substance to the view that more or less 'urban' or 'rural' positions on a continuum are linked to consistent variations in social organization, economic function or set of cultural values. There is, in other words, no universal urban structure or way of life; from which it may be inferred that Wirth's ideal-typical urbanism is of little heuristic value. In parallel with this line of argument is the erosion of claims that urban spatial forms generate common patterns of social life. For Gans (1968) there is little substantive evidence in support of any connection between supposedly urban 'spatial' relations and some specific pattern of social outcomes. In this sense there is no universal social ecology either.

The failure to produce a generic definition of the city is not so much the result of some inexplicable logical error in urbanist discourse, as the outcome of an increasing awareness of heterogeneity in what are conventionally regarded as 'urban' forms. This process of increased awareness of 'urban' variation is already evident in the shift in Marx's position between the *German Ideology* and *Pre-Capitalist Economic Formations*, in

Weber's tacit abandonment of the search for a generic definition
of the city in favour of an evaluative yardstick based on the
occidental city, as the city proper (Weber, 1968, pp. 1226–7),
and in Braudel's more recent abandonment of the question of
what all cities hold in common, in favour of a typology of distinct
'urban' forms. While Fidel Castro once remarked that the city is
a cemetery of revolutionaries, Philip Abrams (1978, p. 9) has
gone on to point out that urban sociology and urban history have
both been graveyards for the idea that 'a town is a town'.

Such arguments suggest that very real confusion may arise
when using terms like 'city' and 'countryside' in a trans-historical
and cross-cultural context. This kind of procedure can create the
misleading implication that all those entities described as 'city'
have some connection with Western conceptions of urbanism as
impersonal *Gesellschaft* or as an historic bearer of innovation,
civilization and social change. The obverse implication that all
entities described as 'countryside' are to be seen as centres of
backwardness, involution, and conservatism on the presumed
Western model of medieval, peasant, natural economy is equally
misleading.

The generic notion of city survives uneasily, therefore, as an
ungrounded conceptual residue in contemporary discussion of
urbanism and urbanization. Its resilience is in fact remarkable in
view of the powerful logical and empirical objections that have
been made to ideas of some universal quality that cities possess
across time and space. The apparently discredited generic sense
of the city as harbinger of civilization refuses to wither away in
spite of its exposure as a contingent feature of Western social
thought. This resilience is very significant and requires further
explanation. Part of the reason is connected with the striking
visual presence of cities. Harris and Ullman (1945, p. 7) reflect
this in their observation that 'as one approaches a city and notices
its tall buildings rising above the surrounding land and as one
continues into the city and observes the crowds of people
hurrying to and fro past stores, theatres, banks and other estab-
lishments, one naturally is struck by the contrast with the rural
countryside'. Within the Islamic word, Ira Lapidus (1969, p. 60)
connects the Muslim 'mystique of cities' and the long-inspired
scholarly quests for that decisive property which unifies Muslim

towns to a similarly visual image of the walled town standing in
relief against a shapeless countryside. For Giddens, too, it is the
city walls and 'physically impressive religious and government
buildings' which do so much to consolidate a generic notion of
city across a range of what he calls all class-divided societies
(1981, p. 146). Visual perceptions it seems still stand as some
kind of barrier against acceptance of the possibility that what is
perceived as city represents a piece of reification or misplaced
concreteness.

Another reason for the resilience of generic forms of urbanist
discourse is connected with the symbolic or metaphysical significance which has become attached to such terms as city and
countryside. Raymond Williams (1975) has pointed out that the
language of 'city and countryside' has served as a means of
symbolizing the key opposition between 'change' and 'continuity', 'future' and 'past', and one might add 'society' and
'nature' in Western thought. Such symbolic associations are not,
however, based on any strict functional correspondence over
time between all the phenomena that are labelled 'urban' or
between all 'rural' entities. For Williams the 'real history' of city
and countryside is characterized by massive diversity. Cities
appear variously as 'state-capital, administrative base, religious
centre, market-town, port and mercantile depot, military
barracks, industrial concentration', etc. while the country way of
life has involved 'the very different practices of hunters, pastoralists, farmers and factory farmers', organized variously through
the tribe, the manor, the feudal estate, small peasant farming,
the rural commune, the plantation and the state farm.

Given the recurring tendency within Western thought to think
of the city as a civilizing agency compared with the natural
innocence of the countryside, Williams is reluctant to explain this
pattern away as a simple illusion. At the same time he can find no
solid grounds for regarding all cities as empirically dynamic or
progressive compared with the 'backward' countryside. What
remains therefore is a strong sense of the metaphorical nature of
terms like 'city' and 'countryside' which stand as mythical symbols rather than concepts with some consistent empirical
reference. For Western thought, then, the contrast of city and
countryside is seen as a symbolic means of formulating 'an unre-

solved division and conflict of impulses' (ibid., p. 357) between the excitement and insecurity of contemplating future change and the conservative yet secure sense of a known past. As Williams notes it might be better all round to face up to such conflicts in their own terms.

Williams feeds into the more general challenge posed in recent social thought to the use of the notion of city and urban/rural difference as a generic structure of cross-temporal and cross-cultural developmental significance. The corollary of this argument is that the elusiveness of the quest for such a generic entity is testimony to the impossibility of the enterprise itself. Where then does this leave the problem of city (and countryside) in the transition to capitalism? Having rejected the universalistic notion of city *sui generis*, should the concept of the city itself be exorcized from what has hitherto been termed urban history and urban sociology, as Philip Abrams (1978, p. 10) has recently suggested.

Abrams' case for so doing rests on the proposition that the 'urban' and 'rural' should be understood as dramatic representations or concentrated manifestations of some more fundamental social relationship rather than as *sui generis* and hence autonomous entities. Most contemporary critics of the generic notion of city have not, however, followed Abrams in this radical step. They have argued instead that the autonomous city, discrete urban social classes and striking urban/rural contrasts can be located as important empirical features of a particular phase in world history. This has generally been associated with late medieval and early modern European history. Whatever else may be said about what are conventionally termed cities at other points in time and space, it remains valid in this view to treat the autonomous occidental city as a *sui generis* feature of Europe in transition from pre-capitalist to modern capitalist social relationships. This conceptual strategy enables urbanism and urban social actors to be posited as causal influences on social change in their own right. But it also leaves open the possibility that there may be a hierarchy of causal influences at work in which cities, while autonomous, may none the less be related to some even more fundamental causally significant social force.

The discontinuity between such views and those of earlier writers like Marx and Weber is in one sense not very great. In his interpretation of Marx on the city, for example, Henri Lefebvre argues that:

> For Marx, the dissolution of the feudal mode of production and the transition to capitalism is attached to a *subject*, the town. The town breaks up the medieval system (feudalism) . . . the town is a 'subject' and a coherent force, a partial system which attacks the global system and which . . . destroys it. (Lefebvre, 1972, p. 71)

Here the logic and contradiction within modes of production occupies the most fundamental place in the hierarchy of causal agencies, with towns occupying a lower order but still fundamentally discrete position. The implication is that the analysis of transition still requires a concept of 'town'. Weber's analysis may be thought of in a similar manner, in that the occidental city is both part of a more general pattern of relations of domination, and yet at the same time a causal influence in its own right.

There are three somewhat distinct versions of the argument linking autonomous cities, and especially urban/rural differences with the process conceptualized by Marxists and some Weberians as the transition from the feudal to the capitalist mode of production. In the first, the urban/rural distinction is seen as characteristic only of the feudal mode of production. Here cities are argued to have played a progressive role within feudalism, thereby creating one of the principal institutional bases for the subsequent transition to capitalism (Pickvance, 1976). In the second, the transition process itself is regarded in terms of an opposition between 'backward' countryside and 'progressive' cities (Lefebvre, 1972). In the third, the capitalist mode of production, at least within its early phases of consolidation, is seen in terms of a confrontation between urban-industrial capitalism and pre-capitalist 'rural' agriculture (Saunders, 1981). In each of these variants, there is the further implication that urban/rural distinctions become gradually undermined once the respective historical phases in question are terminated. Hence for Pickvance, urban/rural distinctions are no longer present once capitalism has emerged, while for Saunders such distinctions are seen as crucial precisely during the early phases of capitalist development, but not so much thereafter.

Abrams' call for the abandonment of the town (and by implication the countryside too) is then a far more radical step than most comparative historical sociologists and historians have been prepared to take. So long as any generic definition of the city as a universally valid causal variable is avoided, it is claimed that the notion of 'city' remains an appropriate component of the analysis of the particular historical conjuncture of European transition to capitalism. This leaves open two possibilities with respect to the conceptual status of the city. The first is to regard the Western city as a unique historical phenomenon of causal significance *qua* 'city' within a delimited sphere of occidental history. The second is to designate the city as an object of inquiry appropriate to urban history rather than urban sociology (Saunders, 1981).

The first of these options may seem logically preferable to the second. Unless 'history' is taken to be a collection of discrete antiquarian exhibits, it is difficult to see how any urban 'history' of particular case studies could subsist without an urban 'sociology' founded on the conceptualization of what is meant by 'urban'. Any notion of the city as a historical object *per se* requires just the same logical specification of what common properties justify the labelling of individual phenomena as cities, as applies in sociological discourse. What is required is not a conceptually incoherent and barren 'urban history' of unique instances but an assessment of the coherence and empirical plausibility of the distinctive delimited developmental properties claimed for the occidental city. It remains difficult to see, however, how analysis of the supposedly unique features of the occidental city can be regarded as a form of urban sociology *per se*, without benefit of a generic definition whereby the 'cities' of the non-Western world could be identified as possessing common properties with those of the West. The problem here is not, therefore, the ideal-typical character of concepts like Weber's 'occidental city' but rather the difficulty of regarding any phenomenon outside of the West as a 'city' proper. The conceptual part of Abrams' challenge remains, namely that the absence of a coherent generic definition of city renders comparative urban sociology incoherent. Instead of the confusing procedure of comparing the occidental city (that is, the city proper) with the supposed 'non-cities' of the non-Western world, we should be identifying the higher-order generic relations which would permit more intelligible comparisons between such phenomena.

Abrams' challenge to 'urbanist' theorists of transition is therefore ultimately conceptual and theoretical, rather than empirical. However important it may be to investigate how much or how little autonomy was possessed by European cities and the burger classes in the transition to capitalism, it still remains to establish the more fundamental patterns of social relations with which ostensibly urban or 'rural' phenomena are coterminous.

3

Urbanist theories of transition to capitalism

Modern theories connecting cities with civilization, progress and freedom have their origins, as we have seen, in a diffuse set of influences deriving from the ancient Mediterranean world and from Western Christianity. The more specific relationship between cities and socio-economic change was not articulated in any elaborate way until the eighteenth century. Two interlocking processes were important at this time. The first was the growing sense of economic activity as both a self-subsistent and a dynamic feature of social life, distinct from systems of government. The second involved an increasing realization that the land no longer represented the overwhelmingly predominant material foundation of human existence. The combined effect of such developments was to connect a belief in the importance of economic determination in history with the agency of non-landed social institutions, whether city or state, as progressive influences for social change.

The emergence of a historical sociology linking cities with the transition to capitalism is located less in discussions of sovereignty and citizenship within political theory and jurisprudence than in the eighteenth century Enlightenment discourses of political economy and conjectural history. Schorske (1963) has connected the early phases of such urbanist explanations of social change with the work of Voltaire, and, more importantly Adam Smith.

ADAM SMITH

Adam Smith's comments on cities, urban/rural differences and their connection with the 'progress of opulence' and the emergence of commercial society represent some of the most important and influential statements of the urbanist explanation of transition. In Book 3 of *Wealth of Nations* (1976) Smith elaborates many themes that have reappeared in more recent debates, such as the cultural divisions between merchant and landowner, the urban origins of much landed improvement, and above all the autonomy of the European city from the surrounding countryside. Underlying these propositions is an emphasis on certain unique features of European social development compared with social change elsewhere.

Smith's point of departure is the deviation of the European developmental experience from a more general model in which economies progress in order through a sequence of agriculture, manufactures and foreign commerce. The logic of this sequence is related to rational choices in which investors tend to avoid risk, preferring the land to industry or domestic trade to foreign trade. Although he sees this model operating to a greater or lesser extent in all situations, Smith also emphasizes the increasing tendency of European societies to develop lead sectors in foreign commerce and manufacture organized by urban mercantile groups. While agriculture, manufacture and trade are always interdependent and make their own sectoral contributions to economic development, Smith emphasizes the importance of 'the commerce of the towns' to the 'improvement of the country'. In the Western case, therefore, dynamic mercantile capital plays the predominant part in transforming agriculture and landed society.

The causal mechanisms at work here include the importance of urban markets as outlets for rural production and incentives to agricultural commercialization, and the investment of urban capital in the countryside. More fundamental forces are seen as underlying these processes. Smith places particular emphasis on the greater liberty and individual security of the urban population compared with the dull servility of the countryside. The argument here combines three discrete points. The first is that the countryside under the domination of territorial lords was indeed a milieu in which liberty was denied. The second is the older notion of the city as a centre of juridical freedom from feudal or seigneurial bonds, guaranteed very often by monarchical authority. For Smith, 'Order and good government and along with them the liberty and security of individuals were in this manner, established in cities at a time when the occupiers of land in the country were exposed to every sort of violence' (Smith, 1976, p. 405). The third element in Smith's argument depends less on the juridical status of towns which he sees as 'corporate' than on the development of an interdependent division of labour between specialized economic actors with the urban milieu. This practice of 'commerce and manufacture' is itself seen as contributing towards 'the liberty and security of individuals'.

The historical genesis of economic individualism is linked therefore with the 'urban milieu'. This is seen, however, not as a causal influence in its own right, but as a concentrated expression of the 'silent and insensible' progression of the division of labour. Different types of social actors have a progressive or conservative effect, therefore, dependent on the centrality of their involvement with commerce and the division of labour. It is this that explains the contrast in mentalities between urban mercantile profit-seeking and risk-taking compared with the consumption-oriented rentier outlook of the country gentleman.

Smith does not deny the importance of agrarian improvement or the development of industries like cloth-making as an offshoot or agriculture. He does, however, maintain that any rural improvement that did eventuate was either the work of urban capital buying into the land, or an unintended consequence of landowners' attempts to maximize consumption incomes by squeezing tenants. Whereas 'great' proprietors acted solely to gratify 'childish vanity', merchants and artificers are seen as operating with a view to their own interest. It is this latter orientation that Smith approves as the cultural basis for his system of 'natural liberty'. This is founded not on explicit commitments to public welfare as in the policies of mercantilist states, but on the rational self-interest of sovereign individuals in the market-place. Given Smith's normative commitment to such a system, it is perhaps not surprising that little further attempt is made to establish the relative importance of endogenous 'great proprietor' improvements compared with those sponsored by urban capital. Nor is it surprising, on the basis of Smith's conceptions of rural servitude, deriving in part from a view of Highland

Scottish life, that little or no attention is given to small agrarian proprietors or petty commodity production in the countryside. In the final analysis, therefore, the role of rural classes in economic change disappears in favour of a bold urbanist formulation to the effect that 'the commerce and manufacture of cities, instead of being the effect, is rather the cause and occasion of the improvement and cultivation of the country' (Smith, ibid., p. 422).

This argument is consolidated empirically by Smith's emphasis on the developmental importance of mercantile cities located on trade routes dependent on sea-borne or river transport. Such cities were not heavily dependent on the immediate agricultural hinterland in so far as their prosperity was related to commerce and manufacture of imported raw materials. They could therefore coexist with a neighbouring countryside whose condition remained largely poverty-stricken. Smith took the mercantile cities of northern Italy, notably Venice, Genoa and Pisa, as the first major examples of this type of urban dynamic.

Historically then, Smith locates the origins of this shift towards commercial society within late medieval and early modern Europe rather than ancient classical times. The main obstruction to economic development in ancient Greece and Rome was the political constraints exercised on both commerce and agrarian development. These included prohibition of the export of corn, taxation of goods in transit, and special restrictive privileges granted to markets and fairs. The fall of the Roman Empire and the erosion of political controls, however, gave no immediate boost to trade. This was due, according to Smith, to the servile or quasi-servile status in which urban traders and artisans still found themselves. The natural tendency to 'truck, barter and exchange' did not then spontaneously assert itself during the early medieval period.

Smith's historical account remains somewhat obscure as to why this urban servility was subsequently broken down in late medieval times. For the most part he is content simply to specify the juridical mechanisms whereby urban merchants established a degree of legal and political autonomy from traditional jurisdiction. There is no suggestion that market-based commerce can undermine political restrictions upon commercial liberty by spontaneous means. In this way the important question of the origins of mercantile towns on which much else depends remains unclear and for later scholars to debate.

Smith's argument about cities and social change is quite clearly located within the spheres of 'conjectural history' and political economy rather than the classical political theory from which such disciplines grew. Thus his belief in the newly emergent commercial society as a system of natural liberty owes comparatively little to classical discussions of the forms of polity best able to engender the moral and aesthetic virtues of public life. Liberty and the conditions for its realization cannot be conceived in isolation from the economic relationships into which the individuals enter. It is inconceivable for Smith that it could be entertained, as with the ancients, while economic servitude remains intact. Unlike classical thinkers his analysis of economic life is neither dominated by the operations of private households (the *oikos*), nor do economic goals remain a secondary adjunct to the achievement of political virtues. Economic life centred on labour and free exchange of the products of labour is rather the centre-point of Smith's normative system of economics. This is further reinforced by his commitment to a version of the labour theory of value as an explanation of the way in which exchange of commodities is made commensurable and legitimate. For Smith, the passions, such as self-love, take precedence over the 'moral sentiments'.

The provenance of Smith's analysis within political economy rather than classical political philosophy introduces a number of important themes in modern discussions of cities and social change. In the first place, when Smith speaks of 'city' and city/ countryside distinctions he does not refer to generic social entities defined by political or cultural characteristics. He does not wish to use city to connote progress and countryside backwardness, nor does he argue that urban civilization somehow endured through ancient, medieval and modern times. His interest is rather in the spatial location of different components of the division of labour, and in the contingent historical connection between the mercantile cities of late medieval Europe and certain political and juridical encouragements to economic freedom. His analyses say very little about the detailed historical evolution of the European *Bürgertum* or bourgeoisie except where their activities intersect with the development of an extended division of labour and the emergence of commercial society. The transition to modern society is not then coterminous with the history of the city or with the historical trajectory of urban social classes.

A second very important theoretical consideration underlies Smith's lack of concern for the city as a generic social entity of developmental significance. This involves the universalism which Smith locates in market relations, whereby the liberty of sovereign individuals is safeguarded against ascriptive ties of social status and the arbitrary deployment of power. For Smith, the individuals who enter market relations are proprietors of their own self-interest and hence on an equal footing. Membership of status rankings whether noble or bourgeois makes no logical difference to this. There is, in other words, no intrinsic difference between the participation of urban or rural actors in the market-place. Somewhat paradoxically, therefore, Smith's universalism implies (for he does not say as much) that the corporate medieval urban institutions, which helped to secure the juridical autonomy of the late medieval city, are incompatible with the market as a system of natural liberty.

LATE EIGHTEENTH AND EARLY NINETEENTH CENTURY POLITICAL THEORY

This universalistic thrust which underlies Smith's analyses and which tends to dissolve the city as a specific component of modern (or commercial) society is paralleled in the late eighteenth and early nineteenth century development of political theory. Here the thrust of democratic movements for popular political sovereignty, associated above all else with the French Revolution, was to erect the individual citizen, rather than the bourgeois as such, as the foundation of the new political order. This in turn reflects the demise of both the older urban communes and those late medieval and early modern political systems based on representation of a hierarchy of status-conscious estates (*Standestaat*). Whereas under such systems the urban burghers had participated as a collectivity in various forms of government and law, in the new system of nation-states the notion of political liberty and citizenship was increasingly freed from ascriptive connotations, especially those that derived from the corporatist status-ridden past. Thus in order to be a citizen, it was not necessary – at least in theory – to be a burgher. The rural dweller was equally as eligible as the town dweller.

The distinction between a democratic polity based on equality of individual subjects before the state and the earlier *Standestaat* system in which *Bürgertum* was constituted as a privileged estate is more clearly represented in French than in German social thought. While the late eighteenth century French vocabulary contained a distinction between *citoyen* (citizen) and 'bourgeois', such linguistic categories were not available in German (Riedel, 1975). Such terms as *Bürgertum* (town dweller) and *Bürgerliche Gesellschaft* (literally, associated of individual town dwellers) conflated both notions of universalistic citizenship and of bourgeois status. The result has been an enduring ambiguity as to what exactly is being claimed in analyses which stress the importance of the European *Bürgertum* or of *Bürgerliche Gesellschaft* in the making of modern Western society, and more especially capitalism. Are such terms as *Bürgertum* or *Bürgerliche Gesellschaft* being used in the sense of a civil society of individual actors engaged in modern economic, political or professional roles, in which case the burgher connotation is logically misleading? Or are they being used to indicate the essentially urban character of modern society and its immediate historical forebears? The ambiguity and confusion that arises from this situation is evident not only in late eighteenth and early nineteenth century German thought as Riedel (1975) has demonstrated, but also in more recent twentieth-century contributions to the analysis of cities and the transition to Western capitalism.

In the epoch of the French Revolution, the universalistic claims associated with the institutions of individual citizenship and the nation-state tended to emphasize the corporatist and particularistic nature of the city and urban social institutions. This was not immediately clear at the outset, when Sièyes' famous pamphlet 'What is the Third Estate' had linked liberty and freedom with the classical legacy of ancient Rome and its Gallic province rather than with rural Germanic life with its traditions of equality between warrior-settlers. It was none the less the privileged rights of aristocrats claiming decent from Frankish conquerors originating 'from the woods and swamps of ancient Germany' that Sièyes challenged. The Third Estate was not an estate at all, but rather all citizens lacking legal privilege but subject to the common law of the nation (Sièyes, 1963, pp. 59–61). This conception of citizenship depended on a theory of natural rights. It was this rationale, rather than any specifically bourgeois identification, that led the French revolutionaries to abolish all corporate privileges, allowing no particular distinction between urban and rural populations within the body of the 'people'.

There are affinities between this position and that of Hegel. In his 'Philosophy of Right', Hegel had reinstated a distinction between city and countryside in his discussion of 'family', 'civil society' and the 'state'. Hegel however regarded city and countryside as insufficiently universalistic compared with the state. He wished to contrast *both* the countryside as the 'seat of ethical life resting on nature and the family', *and* the towns as the sphere of corporate privilege, including business privilege, with the higher universality of the state standing above all such particularities (Hegel, 1952). For Hegel it was the rational Western state as a unity of town and country, rather than any particularly striking urban uniqueness, which represented the important contrast between dynamic occidental civilization and the stationary state of the Asiatic world beyond. In the latter situation, the self-sufficient immolation of villages in caste traditionalism fractured any relationship with the state and the wider society.

Hegel's analysis of social development differs from Smith's in two important respects. First, he places greater emphasis on the guidance of public policy and universalistic public servants in securing social change. Unlike Smith, Hegel does not accept that the extension of the division of labour, concentrated at certain key points in cities and constituted on the basis of rational self-interest, is sufficient to explain the emergence of modern society. For Hegel, following the lead of Sir James Steuart, another Scottish Enlightenment political economist (Plant, 1973), public policy intervention is necessary to ensure the integration of society in the face of dislocating social innovation.

Compared with Smith, Hegel's contribution to the analysis of European transition demands more attention be given to the origins and development of the modern state rather than the division of labour or the occidental city.

Secondly, however, Hegel maintains a more powerful distinction between the world-view of the town and that of the countryside than anything found in Smith. Both sectors are seen by Hegel as involved in business through the deployment of capital as private property. The agricultural class, however, works and depends on nature in a largely self-subsistent way, owing comparatively little to 'reflection and independence of will'. This contrasts with Hegel's view of the urban 'business class' as involved in a socially mediated activity where 'reflection and intelligence' is required to integrate 'one man's needs and work with those of others'. Whereas agricultural classes are seen as embedded in the natural world, directly consuming what they produce, business classes are seen as members of society defined by social exchange.

Although Hegel did not thereby elevate the town/country division into a major causal influence in the development of European society, he does contribute to a view of agrarian life as somehow less socialized than the urban sector. Whereas Smith tended to see rural populations as potentially rational individual actors held back only by feudal repression of liberty, Hegel sees them as contributing 'ethical' rather than economic inputs to social development as synthesized within the universal state. This notion of the lesser socialization of the countryside became even more marked in later nineteenth century thought. By this time the Enlightenment perception of agriculture as a progressive development beyond mere pastoralism or the spontaneous enjoyment of the fruits of nature, involving a measure of human artifice, vied with a far more blatant urbanist hagiography which saw the countryside as a pre-social repository of natural virtues or vices.

MARX

Nineteenth-century thought was never entirely to resolve the tension between a view of the countryside as a natural economy

or conservative order, and the more historically informed realization that rural sectors characterized by agriculture represented a historical progression beyond earlier forms of
hunter-gathering and pastoralism. This tension was manifest in
the coexistence of dichotomous and serial views of history. The
first, as represented in notions of natural economy vs. exchange
economy or *Gemeinschaft* vs. *Gesellschaft* could be neatly
joined with assumptions that towns were dynamic agents of
modernity compared with the developmentally backward
countryside. The second, as represented in the Marxist series of
primitive communist, Asiatic, ancient, feudal and capitalist
modes of production (Marx, 1965b), implied a far more
complex historical process in which such dynamic historical
development as agrarian social differentiation, the emergence
of private property and of the state, all pre-dated the transition
from feudalism to capitalism. This approach recognizes the
existence of pre-capitalist as well as capitalist processes of social
change while leaving considerable scope for variations in urban
or rural contributions to social development within the various
modes of production.

There is a sense in which Marx's comments on the specific
problem of transition from feudalism to capitalism begin where
Smith left off. While Marx reconceptualizes the nature of the
modern European economy as capitalist rather than merely
commercial, his notion of the capitalist mode of production in
the early works is founded, like Smith's, on exchange relations
(*Verkehr*) and the division of labour. In the *German Ideology*,
town/country distinctions are linked to the division of labour
between industrial/commercial and agricultural labour, and the
distinction between capital and landed property. Whereas the
town connotes mental labour and movable capital dependent
only on labour and exchange, however, the countryside connotes
manual labour and immovable property which need to be
dependent on exchange. It is on this basis that Marx attributes a
progressive quality to cities, for in them is concentrated the range
of newly differentiated economic, political and cultural functions
not present in the original agrarian situation. The social differentiation represented by the town extends to 'the necessity of
administration, police, taxes, etc., as well as the concentration of

the instruments of production, of capital, of pleasures [and] of needs (Marx and Engels, 1976, p. 72).

Like Smith, Marx viewed the European city as the locus of civilization. This is expressed not simply in the existence of a division of labour dependent on market exchange, but in the conditions of relative political freedom from feudal contexts emanating from the countryside. At some points Marx and Engels went far beyond Smith in implying a continuity between the European cities of the late Middle Ages and previous epochs. This impression is given in the claim that 'the contradiction between town and country begins with the transition from barbarism to civilisation, from tribe to state, from locality to nation, and runs through the whole history of civilisation to the present day' (ibid., p. 72). At other times, Marx follows Smith in emphasizing the discontinuity between the medieval city and what went before. In his account of the origins of medieval towns, for example, he stresses that they were 'formed anew' by runaway serfs, who required communal institutions for military defence and economic protection to consolidate and secure permanent freedom. They did not derive 'ready-made from an earlier period'.

It is possible to reconcile the apparent discord between Marx's competing notions of urban continuity and discontinuity by locating the differing levels of generality on which they operate. The idea of urban continuity involves a very general hypothesis about cities as indices of social differentiation against which the progress of society may, according to Marx, be measured. The idea of urban discontinuity on the other hand refers to a more specific historical thesis concerning the particular origins of medieval European towns. The two theses are therefore compatible in the sense that the former deals with the general criteria by which particular societies may be evaluated as more or less 'advanced', while the latter deals with specific pathways of social change in a particular historical context. Sahlins has labelled these two different types of exercise as 'the general theory of evolution' and the 'specific theory of evolution' (Sahlins *et al.*, 1960, pp. 23–8).

Marx's early contributions to the theory of transition to capitalism give considerable emphasis to European cities and merchant capital in the development of the new mode of production characterized by a market-based extension of the division of labour. In his later work, as evidenced in the *Grundrisse* and, above all, *Capital*, these emphases are subsumed within a more complex discussion. The principal conceptual innovation here is the insertion of the division of labour into a more fundamental generic framework concerning 'property rights' as they articulate the relations of production.

In his analysis of transition to capitalism, seen now as a distinct system of production relations dependent on wage labour, Marx focuses his historical discussion on relations of production within feudalism. Particular emphasis is placed on the process of 'primary accumulation' whereby serf or peasant labour is detached from ties with the soil to become available as wage labour. This line of analysis helps Marx to address a major weakness in trade-based explanations of the emergence of capitalism, namely that historical experience showed markets and the commodification of the exchange of goods and services to be perfectly consistent with non-capitalist relations of production. The argument was quite simply that without the commodification of labour power, which at the outset meant rural labour power, the existence of urban mercantile capital would be insufficient by itself to secure transition to capitalism.

Marx reached such conclusions only after further analysis of city/countryside relations within different modes of production. In his notebooks of the late 1850s translated as *Pre-Capitalist Economic Formations*, Marx formulates the key statement already cited (see above, p. 20) in which he differentiates between the nature of city/countryside relations within different modes of production. History is no longer represented as a dichotomy between progressive cities and the backward or barbaric countryside. In the case of the ancient mode of production, for example, Marx now links classical history with cities based on landownership and agriculture, themselves dependent on slavery. The implication is that the Roman Empire, for all its trading activity, did not secure the transition to capitalism due to the lack of differentiation between private and communal property rights. The foundation of the ancient cities on landownership and agriculture is not indicative of wealthy developed cities *per se*, as of insufficiently developed private property rights capable of generating commodification of labour power and the erosion of landed immobility. Despite appearances to the contrary, the ancient city functions here not as an urban structure *sui generis* but rather as a symbol for a particular configuration of property rights. While Marx speaks of the ruralization of the ancient city, this is more appropriately interpreted as the mediation of private property through the community of the *polis* of landowners.

In the case of the feudal mode of production, Marx goes on to define a somewhat paradoxical situation where the Middle Ages start with a countryside as the locus of history but then experience a dynamic opposition between city and countryside. In this discussion there is no warrant in Marx for regarding the city as an autonomous agency or the historic subject of this process of change. Rather he uses the town/country opposition to symbolize a distinction between relations of production based on society and relations of production based on nature.

In a manner broadly similar to Hegel's distinction between the milieux of the agricultural and business classes, Marx's notion of society stands for sociality embracing production and exchange mediated through human consciousness and purpose. Nature, meanwhile, stands for an unmediated isolated connection between humanity and the land. Without any further empirical investigation of rural social relations, Marx stereotypes the European countryside as a domain characterized by producers vegetating in an organic connection with the soil. Where Marx clearly challenges Hegel is in the notion that the state represents a universalism standing above civil society, that is, *Bürgerliche Gesellschaft*. For Marx it is the extension of the domain of civil society over nature, and the social contradictions brought about as a result, that create the basis for transition to a more universalistic sociality and social order. This involves the 'socialization' (read urbanization) of 'nature' (read countryside), through the development of a fully socialized mode of production and class structure. Thus instead of looking to the state or to abstract citizenship rights, Marx continues to focus on the immense developmental significance or urban/rural differences and the progressive significance of capitalist development in furthering social development towards a more universalistic social order.

In *Grundrisse* Marx falls back on trade and exchange as the major solvents of rural society. Here the forces of the transition to capitalism impact on feudalism from outside. This is not surprising given the way rural social relations are characterized as an anathema to change. Towns continue to be regarded as external to feudalism, acting as immanent agents of the development of wage labour and capitalist development. In *Capital*, however, the emphasis has changed.

Marx's discussion of primary accumulation in *Capital* (1965a) emphasizes the importance of property rights and class struggles generated over the exercise of those rights within feudalism. The stress here is on *internal* class struggles within feudalism and their importance for the erosion of serfdom and the release of labour from ties to the feudal estate. Anxious to combat those historians who viewed the development of British society as a gradual and peaceable 'ever onward and upward' progression, Marx stressed the violent and conflict-ridden nature of social change involving 'blood and fire.' While aware of the flow of urban capital into the land, Marx, in his analysis of the pioneering transition to capitalism in England, gives pride of place to mechanisms whereby former feudal aristocrats increasingly entered commodity markets in the tenth century. Land was increasingly treated as capital and peasants were uprooted, according to Marx, to make way for commercial production.

A good deal of the analysis rests on the specific case of enclosures connected with the development of the English wool trade. However typical of the general pattern of transition this case study may be (or whether there is some such general pattern at all), what is most noteworthy about Marx's comments for present purposes is the shift away from any prominent reference to urban/rural opposition. This is now replaced by a complex discussion of interaction between changes in rural property relations, the relocation of much urban industry in the countryside to escape guild restrictions, and the expansion of world markets, a process itself connected with European geographical discoveries in the early modern period. As Marx himself pointed out, modern capitalism generally began outside the old corporate towns, characterized by monopolistic guild restrictions, very often within rural putting-out industries, organized by merchant-manufacturers. It is not clear what, if anything, such processes owed to the older urban communes composed in Marx's view of runaway serfs. Nor is it clear how rural producers managed to throw off the traditional organic ties with nature to participate in the putting-out system, and whether there may be autonomous non-urban origins of agrarian capitalism.

What is certain is that Marx no longer believed that trade and towns themselves created a sufficient dynamic to produce a transition to capitalism. But beyond this fundamental but very general proposition all else remains unresolved. No general theory of transition emerges from *Capital*, least of all one founded on urban/rural differences. Much on the contrary appears historically contingent, as in the English case, on developments like the impact of the dissolution of the monasteries on the land market.

Whatever beneficial influences Marx's more general conceptual armoury may have had on the analysis of social change, it remains the case that his shifting and unresolved comments on cities and capitalism could not be taken much further without far greater attention to empirical analysis. In Marx's case as with Smith, too much remains speculative. While subsequent scholars have added few new interpretative themes to those already broached, further advances in the controversy over cities and the making of modern Europe were to depend on the evaluation of a mass of archival evidence, leading to the empirical grounding of hitherto conjectural hypotheses. The advent of empirical historiography did not, however, entirely erode the mythical element in European thought concerning the city and civilization.

Late nineteenth and early twentieth century debates on the origins and developmental significance of European cities engaged a wide range of historians, legal theorists and historical economists. The leading question for many concerned the origins of town settlements rather than any connection between cities and the making of modern society. The former question generated many rival interpretations, pitting 'Romano-Gallic' theories of continuity between ancient and medieval urban institutions against Germanic theories of gradualist urban development from 'free' village communities.

The question of origins was none the less connected with theories of social change and the historical evolution of Western society. Karl Bücher, the German historical economist, for example, developed a three-stage model of this process organized around the basis of exchange between producer and consumer. This featured the 'stage of independent domestic economy', where producers consume what they produce, 'the stage of town economy' (*Stadtwirtschaft*) where goods pass directly from producer to consumer, and 'the stage of national economy', where a much more complex chain of transactions separated producer and consumer (Bücher, 1968, p. 89). Both Bücher and other influential German historical economists took the medieval cities of Europe to be of crucial developmental significance. In Schmoller's case, they were placed in a category alongside nineteenth-century railways, as two of the decisive forces in the making of modern Europe (cited in Lyon, 1974, p. 64). The enduring influence of the urbanist theory of capitalist development, as it was elaborated by Schmoller's contemporaries and successors, has come to be associated with the two major figures of Henri Pirenne and Max Weber.

PIRENNE AND WEBER

Henri Pirenne, the Belgian economic and social historian, first published a series of papers on the problem of urban origins in the 1880s and 1890s, later consolidating and extending his argument in two important studies, *The Early Democracies of the Low Countries*, first published in French in 1910, and *Medieval Cities*, published in 1925. Max Weber's essay on *The City (Non-Legitimate Domination)* was written around 1910–11 and first published in Germany in 1920. There is no evidence, however, that Weber had been influenced by Pirenne's earlier work, or that Pirenne's study of medieval cities drew in any way on Weber's work. Turner's claim (1981, p. 248) that Pirenne's work represents an attempt 'to develop and apply Weber's perspective on urbanization under patrimonial and feudal conditions' is mistaken.

Pirenne and Weber can both be regarded as representatives of the urban cosmopolitan components of the nineteenth century liberal bourgeois world-view. While Marx had also drawn on the cosmopolitan side of this legacy in elaborating his internationalism, he differed from Pirenne and Weber in calling quite clearly for the transcendence of urban/rural distinctions and class division. His two successors by contrast identified strongly with the economic and political programmes of liberal industrial capitalism, and with the ideals of urban culture. Pirenne, for example, came from a family of Belgian industrialists, whose mixed Walloon, German and Italian background discouraged a commitment to a 'provincial and characteristically Belgian outlook' (Lyon, 1974, pp. 24–5). While deeply aware and proud of the contribution of the Low Countries to liberal political freedom and economic progress, Pirenne retained a strong sense of the essentially European context of the social transformation of the late medieval and early modern period. Cities and the urban culture of nation-states were the carriers of civilization. Weber, for his part, although politically identified with the expansive aims of German imperialism, proudly proclaimed his membership of the bourgeois class. 'I consider myself one and I have been raised according to its views and ideals' (Weber, 1978, p. 263). The cosmopolitan strain in Weber's bourgeois affiliation is to be seen in his rejection of both narrowly Germanic and Romanist views of the dynamics of the European past and present. He subscribed neither to Romantic views of the emergent vitality of the Germanic folk community founded on racist or egalitarian myths, nor to exclusively 'Roman' views of European history preoccupied by continuities between Roman law and government and the modern state. Weber's emphasis, like that of Pirenne, transcends competing national historiographies in its emphasis on the essentially European or occidental character of the bourgeoisie as a distinct social class, and of capitalism itself.

In view of this shared *Weltanschauung* it is not surprising that Pirenne and Weber also advanced many similar substantive historical propositions in their analyses of how the urban component of modern European society first emerged as a dynamic force. Foremost among these is the emphasis on the politico-legal autonomy of the late medieval city as the foundation for an expansion of capitalist social relations. Pirenne, like Smith and

Marx before him, equated trade and the urban mercantile life
with 'liberty', in contrast to the 'servitude' of agrarian civilization. The empirical basis for such comparisons rested on the
rejection of notions of the historical prevalence of a free
peasantry, together with the observation that serfdom had been
quickly abolished in cities. This 'freedom' did not emerge spontaneously, however, but only through conflict between merchants seeking juridical and political autonomy and traditional
rulers. While the political resolution of such conflicts is seen as a
complex matter of historical analysis, Pirenne offers two basic
mechanisms whereby autonomy was achieved. These involve the
'Liège type' where urban privileges were the result of compromise existing side by side with more traditional or feudal
jurisdictions, and the 'Flemish type' where autonomy is more
complete, though usually as a result of the political backing of a
powerful prince.

However complex such processes may have been, Pirenne is
quite clear that it is the advance of urban autonomy that 'rouses
the peasant from his age-old torpor', undermines rural serfdom,
leads to the disappearance of 'the old rural economies' based on
self-subsistence and ties the countryside to dependence on the
urban economy. For Pirenne, as for Weber, 'town air makes
free' in the sense that urban autonomy is represented as a very
real check on feudal jurisdiction. What Pirenne is none the less
anxious to make clear is that such freedom remains privileged
and status-bound and is in no sense equivalent to modern notions
of individual freedom. For all this its developmental significance
for the advance of capitalism is quite evidently positive.

Weber, like Pirenne, emphasizes the politico-legal constitution of urban freedom. With the emergence of the urban
'commune' as a legal entity from the eleventh century onwards, a
community of interest is created among burgers acting to pro-
mote economic as well as political interests, but increasingly free
from ascriptive ties of kinship, clan or caste. Weber summarizes
the autonomous elements of the ideal-typical Western city in
terms of political autonomy, autonomous law creation, auto-
cephaly, taxing autonomy, market rights and autonomous urban
economic policy. Whereas Pirenne explains such developments
on the basis of expanding trade and successful mercantile politi-

cal interventions in defence of economic interest, Weber's analysis emphasizes the voluntaristic usurpation of existing legitimate domination by the burghers. Thus the 'city' for Weber is not so much an entity in its own right as the social arena for a struggle over conflicting principles of traditional and rational-legal domination. Since rational-legal authority is a multi-faceted phenomenon connected with political, juridical and cultural as well as economic features of modern Western society, Weber's explanation does not depend on an underlying economic force lying behind the urban usurpationary bid. His analysis looks further to such causal influences as the confrater-nal legacy of the ancient city, and the individual rather than kin-based provenance of Western Christianity. Even so, Weber is seen to emphasize the contrast between the ancient *polis* as a commune of land-based warriors, and the medieval city as a commune of burghers conceived as arms-bearing economic actors. In other words the medieval city is very far from a simple re-emergence or regeneration of pre-existing ancient institutions.

Weber like Pirenne insisted on the importance of urban/rural differences and their correspondence with spheres of develop-mental dynamism and conservatism. In a manner reminiscent of Marx, Weber also speaks of the restrictions on rural landed property rights where village and manorial claims constrain peasant freedom. This contrasts in his view with the absolute alienability of urban landed property (Weber, 1968, p. 1237). It was left, therefore, for the late medieval urban communes to liberate the countryside by undermining feudal and traditional patterns of domination, thereby eroding constraints on the legiti-mate pursuit of rational economic action expressed through alienable property rights. This in turn stimulated the emergence of free wage labour, as well as creating legitimate space for rational-legal activity in any sphere.

Within the analysis of rural/urban differences, Weber gives a far greater attention to the explicit content and developmental implications of agrarian social relations than does Pirenne. For the latter it was sufficient to demonstrate problems with the Germanic *Landgemeinde* theory which claimed that cities grew organically from free village communities (Lyon, 1974, pp. 176–7). If it could be shown that the European countryside had experienced a consistent history of servitude, Pirenne felt content that his alternative mercantile settlement theory of urban origins could not be challenged on the grounds that it exaggerated urban/rural differences. For Weber, on the other hand, the relationship between relations and social change warranted far greater and more detailed attention, in part because it gave one of the best clues to the problem of why the Roman Empire had not secured a transition to capitalism.

Weber's interest in the agrarian history of Imperial Rome stemmed in part from the question of comparability between the fate of the Roman Empire and that of the contemporary German Empire with its own large agrarian sector currently involved in the nineteenth century German transition to capitalism. Weber, like Marx, perceived that the urban civilization of the ancient Mediterranean world rested on an agrarian base. This had not in itself inhibited the development of capitalism as a system of economic acquisition through market exchange. At the same time the extent of this development was limited by both the essentially manorial basis of agrarian conditions and the dependence on slave labour. These served to limit the development of an extensive division of labour involving a range of market-directed urban producers employing free wage labour. The ancient cities were therefore very much centres of consumption dominated by the rule of a land-based social class. Underlying this restrictive pattern was the political organization of the Empire whose continuing stability was dependent on a constant supply of slaves. Once this was checked, the whole structure became vulnerable to economic and political collapse compounded by administrative difficulties in maintaining a centralized structure. The collapse of the Roman Empire led to an essentially rural social structure during the Middle Ages, close to what Pirenne regarded as a natural economy. The moral for contemporary Germany was to avoid the slave-like deployment of proletarianized labour as had tended to occur on the agricultural estates east of the Elbe, and to combat bureaucratic administrative structures similar to those that had strangled the Roman Empire. For a German liberal bourgeois, however, this did not mean support for *Junker* landowners as a proto-capitalist agrarian class, but rather a policy of settled peasant small farming under urban tutelage.

While Weber's agrarian sociology of the ancient world provides useful insight into the limitations of capitalist development on agrarian foundations within a slave-based Empire, it is less useful in understanding the role of the agrarian sector in the transition to capitalism. It is true that Weber saw the decentralized political structure of feudalism as more vulnerable to usurpatory challenge by merchant classes than would have been the case under centralized imperial administration. He did not, however, analyse the medieval and early modern agrarian sector to assess its potential for capitalist development. This absence may be explained in part by the lack of connection of the dispersed feudal or manorial lords with dynamic features of urban culture. While Weber's urban focus demanded analysis of the land-based citizenry and *polis* of the ancient world, the essentially rural feudalism of the Middle Ages assumed significance only as a negative contrast with what went before. The re-emergence of a dynamic towards capitalism was, as with Marx, associated essentially with the urban arena. In the process Weber left no space for what might be called a Germanic theory of agrarian capitalist development in which social differentiation within the countryside might produce a development from free independent peasant farming to an agrarian capitalism of farmers and wage labourers. For while Weber did accept the notion of an originally free Germanic peasantry, as Pirenne did not, he regarded the activities and world-view of this group as of little developmental interest, given the prevalence of servile manorial domination.

Given the prevailing nationalistic and sometimes racist setting of much late nineteenth century historiography, it is important to stress that Pirenne and Weber shared a belief in the general transnational developmental significance of late medieval cities in different parts of Europe. While Pirenne's more detailed studies dwelt on the experience of the Low Countries and Weber drew in the main on the case study of northern Italy, both sought a general explanatory framework for the nature and function of cities at this time. For Pirenne this involves, as we have seen, a combination of the late medieval revival of trade, and the constitution of urban communal autonomy, while for Weber it is the changing structure of legitimate domination that is most central. In both cases there is no explicit deployment of a conception of urbanity *sui generis*.

The most important divergence between Pirenne and Weber concerns the nature of capitalism, that is the new and dynamic economic system whose emergence is to be explained. For Pirenne, capitalism is defined in terms of 'individual enterprise, advances on credit, commercial profits and speculation' (Pirenne, 1913–14, pp. 495–6), thereby combining relational criteria linked to market exchange of commodities with the orientation of individual actors. Such criteria approximate closely to Marx's notion of merchant capital consistent with different modes of production. They also have some affinity with Weber's conception of age-old capitalism founded on acquisitiveness, although Weber sees this as consistent with corporate and state monopolistic organization in a manner ruled out by Pirenne's liberalistic reference to individuals. Pirenne's definition of capitalism diverges even more markedly, however, from Weber's conception of modern capitalism. For Weber, there is nothing specifically Western about mercantile trade or the acquisitive search for profit as such. It is rather the combination of a new rational orientation to profit-making as a vocation, coupled with structural changes associated with the development of free wage labour and the rational enterprise that constitute the unique features of occidental capitalism. It follows from this that the empirical tests for the presence of 'capitalism' in late medieval cities are somewhat different for Weber than for Pirenne.

One aspect of this difference is the comparative dimension whereby Weber emphasized the distinctiveness of occidental history through a range of social phenomena including both the Western urban commune and modern capitalism. The structure of Weber's argument about cities and capitalism cannot be reduced to internal arguments about European institutions, for it engages with a set of comparative distinctions in the development of world history. Although Weber's argument might be damaged if it could be shown that in the European case urban air was not the main source of modern freedom this would not by itself constitute an adequate rebuttal of the comparative basis of his theory of occidental uniqueness. Provided it could be demonstrated that a uniquely Western mode of modern capitalism did indeed emerge as Weber suggests in the late medieval and early modern period, it would still be necessary to assess the comparative dimension of Weber's cross-cultural historical sociology before abandoning any hypothesis linking Western cities with Western capitalism.

If Weber's emphasis on the rational-legal non-ascriptive basis of Western urban autonomy compared with the cities of the Orient were confirmed, for example, it might still be possible to retain elements of this thesis, while shifting the relative weight of the explanation of modern capitalist development to other unique features of Western history, including the Christian legacy or the decline of Empire, and the rise of the nation-state. Pirenne, by contrast, offers little comparative dimensions to his research beyond the assumption that the Islamic civilizations which had threatened Europe in the epoch of Charlemagne offered a less hospitable environment to trade and capitalism than that which evolved in the free cities of medieval Europe. For Pirenne, it was not until the re-opening of the Mediterranean to trade after the Islamic defeat that the dynamic for capitalist development emerged. Unlike Weber, Pirenne leaves unanswered questions as to the significance of Islamic trade and mercantile activity for the developmental trajectory of Islamic societies. This silence reflects his association of capitalism with economic liberalism, quite distinct from any element of plunder, force or military conquest. As such, the militaristic activities of Islam preoccupy Pirenne at the expense of Islamic economic activity. Weber's distinction between capitalism as acquisition and modern capitalism by contrast allows him to recognize the mercantile achievements of the Islamic world, while at the same time differentiating acquisitive adventurer activity from the rational calculative pursuit of profit as an end in itself, constitutive of the modern Western system. Similarly, Weber's comparative urban sociology permits him to identify in the supposedly clan and sib-based social organization of the Islamic city (Weber, 1968, pp. 1231–4) a possible explanation for the failure of rational-legal urban structures of individual economic actors to emerge.

A further important difference between Pirenne and Weber stemming from their divergent conceptions of capitalism involves the precise relationship proposed in the connection between cities and the transition to capitalism. For Pirenne, late medieval urban autonomy is a component part of a wider set of mercantile institutions which themselves constitute the realization of capitalism – at least in its initial stages. For Weber, by contrast, the link between cities and modern capitalism is more complex. Weber certainly regards the late medieval urban communes as 'the major forerunner of the modern specifically western form of capitalism'. In addition the urban burgher estate is also seen as unique to the West and of major developmental significance. Yet for all this Weber does not explicitly claim that urban autonomy constitutes modern capitalism as such. While aware of the importance of such developments as rational accounting and the differentiation between family and business in the cities of Renaissance Italy (Weber, 1924), he remained impressed by discontinuities of attitude and organization between this period and the more recognizably modern capitalist economies of eighteenth and nineteenth century Europe. At best such cities were transitional between two distinct orders of society. Yet for Weber such transitional status implied no evolutionary necessity whereby forerunners of modernity must lead on to modern capitalism itself.

Such considerations highlight a further important divergence between Pirenne and Weber concerning the theory of social change. Pirenne, like many other European scholars of the pre-1914 epoch, upheld an evolutionary theory of change linked to a view of history as progress. As far as the development of capitalism was concerned, this meant not so much ever onward and upward progression, but a series of ascending stages based successively on city, international trading company and nation-state. At each stage a newly emergent capitalist class was to be seen with origins outside previous dominant classes. In the late medieval setting this involved the formerly peripatetic merchants who settled in the 'port' districts near to protective fortifications or jurisdictions.

While the autonomous urban organizations that they created were eventually to be overtaken from the fifteenth century onwards by international trading companies and the nation-state, the initial dynamic behind the expansion of capitalism as a new social system had been set. While Pirenne did not confine his view of progress to the development of capitalism, believing liberal-democratic freedoms and social welfare reform to be other important components of the process, his overall approach to social change is unambiguously evolutionary.

The characterization of Weber's social change theory and the place of the city within it is far more difficult. A number of unresolved problems continue to mark out this area as a highly controversial one. At one level, it remains uncertain as to whether Weber may be regarded as an evolutionist on the Darwinian model (Langton, 1982) or an adherent of a developmental history in which history is seen as pattern, but as a result of the contingent interplay of causal forces outside the domain of some unfolding teleological process (Roth, 1976). At another level there is dispute between those who see Weber's work in terms of an underlying unity around the rationalization thesis (Tenbruck, 1975) and those who perceive a fragmented open-ended *oeuvre*. Such controversies seem to be less a matter of exegetical disagreement than symptoms of a profound ambivalence in Weber's social change theory. On the one hand, this set out from a neo-Kantian epistemology which rejected any sense of teleological pattern in history on thc model of natural law theory, but, on the other hand, Weber maintained a strongly enthocentric viewpoint in asserting the universal cultural significance of Western history and the processes of social change leading to the rationalization of and disenchantment of the world. The ambivalence here is between an apparent methodological defence of pluralistic readings of history according to varying standards of cultural relevance, and the fateful sense of an underlying unitary historical evolution in the direction of greater rationalization. It is important that such inner tensions are not suppressed in any evaluation of the place of cities in Weber's discussion of transition to capitalism.

It has not always been appreciated, for example, that Weber projected a 'circular' fate for European cities, rather than progressive linear development connecting urban autonomy with capitalism on the model of Pirenne. What this means is that while

urban autonomy did emerge from patrimonial or feudal regimes
for several centuries, it did not lead straight into modern capitalism. Instead the formerly autonomous cities under mercantile
dominance gradually became undermined by closed monopolistic urban patrician elites, and by the development of the absolutist state. While the period between the tenth and thirteenth
centuries had seen the expansion of urban autonomy, the period
between the fourteenth and seventeenth centuries marked its
erosion. As Weber (1961, p. 337) points out:

> The English city of the seventeenth and eighteenth centuries
> had ceased to be anything but a clique of guilds which could lay
> claim only to financial and social class significance. The Ger-
> man cities of the same period, with the exception of the
> Imperial cities, were merely geographical entities (Landstadt)
> in which everything was ordered from above. In the French
> cities this development appeared even earlier . . . The Italian
> cities found themselves in the power of the 'signory'.

How then is Weber's line of argument to be sustained further
in the transition towards capitalist consolidation? It seems that
two mechanisms are possible. In the first case, the late medieval
and early modern experience of urban autonomy left its impact
on the now dominant state, producing as it were capitalism 'from
above'. In the second place, the earlier experience of urban
autonomy was somehow later recovered through some kind of
fusion with the 'spirit of capitalism' to produce, as it were 'capitalism from below'.

Several commentators including Bendix (1966), Saunders
(1981) and Poggi (1983) interpret Weber's position in the second
of these ways. Thus the institutional and ideological legacy of
urban autonomy is seen as paving the way for the subsequent
acceptance of the Protestant ethic and fundamental changes in
the orientation towards economic activity. This position has
been powerfully expressed by Poggi in his claim that:

> the *Protestant Ethic* concerns not so much the formation of a
> wholly new collective actor, as the (however radical) trans-
> formation of a pre-existent one – an urban status group already

involved in the conduct of business, and on this account already possessing a distinctive (and privileged) social location with the early modern city. . .

Poggi's explanation of why the urban theme does not appear in *The Protestant Ethic* is simply that 'Weber took it utterly for granted that the processes he postulated had the early modern city as their locale' (Poggi, 1983, p. 93).

While it is important to emphasize that Western *Bürgertum* and the Protestant Ethic formed two components of Weber's notion of occidental uniqueness, this line of commentary is in some danger of positing a tighter and more unitary urbanist discourse in Weber's historical sociology than is warranted. For Weber, the development of modern Western society depends as much on the emergence of a system of competing nation-states and national bourgeois as it does on the secularization of the Protestant notion of calling through urban individualism acting from below. This is made clear in the *General Economic History* (1961) where Weber argues that:

> The modern city was deprived of its freedom . . . [as it] . . . came under the power of competing national states in a condition of perpetual struggle for power in peace or war. This competitive struggle created the largest opportunities for modern western capitalism. The separate states had to compete for mobile capital, which dictated to them the conditions under which it would assist them to power. Out of this alliance of the state with capital, dictated by necessity, arose the national citizen class, the bourgeoisie in the modern sense of the word. It is the closed national state which accorded for capitalism its chance for development – and as long as the national state does not give place, to a world empire, capitalism also will endure. (ibid., p. 337)

While certain of the forms of rational-legal authority developed within the medieval urban commune were seen by Weber as precursors of the modern state, they cannot be regarded as direct linear forebears of it. The modern state emerges for Weber very much out of the ruins of the urban communes in part out of a rediscovery of the centralized rather than parcellized jurisdiction of Roman Law, and in part as an unintended consequence of the rationalization of European absolutism.

A significant hiatus is therefore detectable between the early modern opoch of the demise of urban autonomy and the eighteenth and nineteenth century development of a system of competing nation-states wherein Weber feels emerged the largest opportunities for modern Western capitalism. When Weber takes up the theme of transition again in this later epoch within the latter part of the *General Economic History* (1961), we are a long way from the urban economic splendour of the Italian Renaissance cities or the petty commodity producers and artisans who formed the audience for Puritan divines like Richard Baxter. The mechanisms of transition to modern Western capitalism now depend on a macro-level alliance between 'state' and 'capital'.

While relatively undeveloped, such themes suggest that Weber's commentary on the transition to Western capitalism cannot be encapsulated within an evolutionary theory of urban-centred social change whereby the Western *Bürgertum* becomes gradually transformed into a modern bourgeoisie. Against Poggi, it may be argued that the reason Weber did not choose to emphasize the urban location of the Protestant inspired spirit of modern capitalism is because he did not see the city or the bourgeoisie as a discrete object of social inquiry exhibiting a clear-cut historical continuity between the late medieval, early modern and modern epochs. In spite of the alliance between capital, the bourgeoisie and the modern nation-state, this latter institution is far more than *Bürgertum* writ large. Weber's emphasis on the contingent interplay of a plurality of elements in Western history, including Christianity and Roman law, in the making of rational-legal authority is obscured when the inner tension in his social change theory is suppressed in favour of an unambiguous evolutionary theory of the unfolding of Western uniqueness.

It is arguable that the work of Pirenne and Webber is impor-tant less for its originality in formulating key components of the urbanist theory of transition, than for its conceptual and empirical elaboration of ideas expressed in rather fragmentary fashion by forerunners like Smith and Marx. This applies both to the strategic historical importance of late medieval cities as solvents of feudalism and traditionalism, and to developmental theories stressing the urban origins of agricultural transformation. While Weber's comparative urban historical sociology was far more ambitious than anything previously attempted, it too draws upon notions of European/oriental contrast tied up with arguments about the city as a unique feature of Western civilization.

It is also arguable that much twentieth-century debate on European cities and transition has the character of a critical commentary on Pirenne and Weber. This applies especially to the celebrated transition debate launched by Dobb and Sweezy, in which Pirenne's researches were deployed by the two protagonists in arguments about the location of cities with respect to juridical and political structures associated with feudal and capitalist modes of production. It is also evident in recent debates on the relative importance of cities in capitalist and socialist societies. Here Weber's comparative framework has been extended to suggest that variations in urbanity may be a critical variation in securing transition to either capitalism or socialism (Szelenyi, 1981). Underlying these controversies is the continuing cultural resonance of the notion that 'town air makes free'. Having secured axiomatic status this has served both as a totem for historical analyses of the developmental dynamism of the West, and as a contemporary call to defend or reassert the idea of free urban space in the face of the restructuring of city centres by private capital, and the expansion of suburban privatization.

This axiomatic status has none the less come under damaging challenge in recent years so as to throw both historical and contemporary political prognoses into confusion and doubt. The 'historical' controversy, which was first thematized in an elaborate way by Dobb, has now reached such proportions as to warrant serious consideration of the most fundamental components of the 'urbanist' case. The critique of this case assembled in the following chapter raises the possibility that a strong autonomous agrarian development coupled with political changes associated with the nation-state should be integrated into the analysis of transition. It further suggests that the notion 'town air makes free' is for the most part an over-inflated piece of historical mythology of relatively minor significance in the explanation of capitalist development.

4
A historical critique of urbanist theory

Controversy over the various urbanist theories of the European transition to capitalism has concentrated on four major areas. These may be listed, in their barest essentials, as follows:

1 *The relationship between European cities and feudal or pre-capitalist social structures*   Are such cities to be regarded as autonomous islands of capitalism in a sea of feudalism, or conversely as structurally and culturally located within pre-capitalist society? Or is this antinomy insufficiently sensitive to a more complex and evolving relationship between cities and transitional forms of social organization?
2 *The relationship between city and countryside in the transition to capitalism*   Do cities and urban social classes induce social change and innovation in an otherwise 'backward' country-side, or are there autonomous sources of change located outside the urban milieu? Can 'rural air make free', while 'urban air' may be resistant to freedom? Is it more appropriate to think in terms of the interdependence between 'urban' and 'rural' sources of transition to capitalism, in which case are the 'urban' and the 'rural' causal variables in their own right or coterminous with other social forces?
3 *The relationship between cities and nation-state formation*   Is there a continuity between the institutions and policies of late medieval cities and those involved in the development of European nation-states? Is the nation-state, the political form in which Western capitalism developed, merely the city and bourgeoisie writ large? Or should it be seen as an autono-mous institution with significant extra-urban roots, irreduci-ble to urban-centred innovation?

4   *Comparisons between cities in the European and non-European worlds*   Is there a contrast between the occidental city and the urban institutions of the non-Western worlds? If so, are such contrasts of developmental significance?

The present chapter will concentrate on the first three of these issues, that is on the internal history of the Occident, leaving broader comparative issues to be debated in Chapter 5.

THE RELATIONSHIP BETWEEN EUROPEAN CITIES AND FEUDAL OR PRE-CAPITALIST SOCIAL STRUCTURES

The proposition that late medieval cities represented 'islands of capitalism' within a surrounding feudal environment is a powerful underpinning of most urbanist theories of transition. The evidence in favour of this proposition is usually taken to include the following:

1   The economic specialization and organizational innovation associated with mercantile and industrial activities within cities, contrasted with functionally undifferentiated agrarian countryside.
2   The upswing of the European economy between 1000–1300 in terms of population growth, increasing production and the development of new markets, contemporaneous with a process of urban expansion.
3   The tendency for urban centres to dispense with serfdom and hence to provide a refuge for serfs escaping from manorial servitude within the feudal countryside.
4   The political and juridical autonomy of most urban centres from feudal jurisdiction, allowing a separate system of law and local government for urban groups.
4   The development of an autonomous *Bürgertum* involving association between individuals, rather than exclusively ascriptive ties based on kinship or personal dependence, characteristic of feudalism.

While it is important to bear mind Hilton's warning that the typical late medieval town was probably closer to the unspectacular settlements of Gloucester or Metz than to more glittering examples such as Venice (Hilton, 1984, p. 90), there is little disagreement that the late medieval period did experience a period of economic upswing, urban expansion and political innovation. Between 1000 and 1340 AD European population increased by nearly 100 per cent, with particularly strong increases being registered in the north, west and in northern Italy (Russell, 1972, p. 36). This itself indicates a capacity to feed many more people than ever before. Meanwhile, by the beginning of the thirteenth century the Italian city-states of Milan, Venice and Florence had each grown to around 100,000 on the basis of long-distance commerce, banking and manufacture (Martines, 1983, p. 230). Flanders, meanwhile, had developed a regional economy based on cloth production and commerce in which around 50 per cent of the populace lived in cities (Braudel, 1973, p. 376). Most observers agree that such urban centres possessed a high degree of cultural self-consciousness as well as economic buoyancy. This was reflected in the enlargement of urban identity and pride, through the construction of churches and public buildings, and, especially in northern Italy, through the emergence of universities as centres of learning.

Nor is there much disagreement that the emerging urban communes of northern Italy and the Low countries represented an important development in political and juridical organization. Such communal organizations may be distinguished both from the imperial model of ancient Rome, and the original feudal bases of settlement whereby invasion and migration saw warrior-bands distribute land on the basis of obligations to provide continuing military service mediated through a hierarchy of personal allegiance. They may also be seen as a good deal more than a revival of the *polis* of free citizens of the ancient city-state. While the ancient *polis* depended to a large degree on slavery and tended to devalue economic activity associated with manual work, the medieval commune became far more intimately connected with economic life through the activities of mercantile and producer guilds and through policies of economic protection of the urban economy. Whatever parallels between the late medieval and ancient worlds emerged with the Renaissance, there can be little doubt that western Europe in 1300 had under-

gone processes of social change significantly different from those
evident within the ancient world and the subsequent epoch of
Germanic invasion.

Major controversies have arisen none the less as to the
developmental significance, and in some cases the empirical
accuracy, of certain key components of the urbanist explanation
of transition to capitalism. One of the most protracted of these
concerns the nature, extent and significance of urban political
juridical and cultural autonomy from feudal, seigneurial and
other traditionalistic structures within late medieval society.
Much of this debate, the period since 1945, has been stimulated
by the important exchange between Dobb and Sweezy over the
exploration of Western capitalist development. (This may be
followed in Dobb (1963) and the collection of articles assembled
in Hilton (1978).)

For Dobb, the expanding late medieval cities of northern Italy
and the Low Countries represented developments internal to
and perfectly consistent with the feudal mode of production.
While Dobb cites Pirenne's work as evidence of the involvement
of centres like Venice and Florence or Ghent and Bruges in
long-distance trade and to a lesser extent manufacturing, he
argues that the basis of economic expansion at this time
remained dominated by mercantile rather than industrial capital.
Mindful of Marx's claim that merchant capital 'is incapable by
itself of promoting and explaining the transition from one mode
of production to another' (Marx, 1959, p. 327), Dobb sees late
medieval merchant capital directed towards the securing of profit
through middle-men or fiscal service functions rather than the
transformation of production methods. In this way small producers were linked with luxury consumers, including landed
aristocrats, while merchant bankers were linked directly with
royal houses and the papacy in the provision of loans. For
Dobb the late medieval urban trading communities remained
'half servants and half parasites upon the body of the feudal
economy' (Dobb, 1963, p. 71).

The claim that late medieval trade, merchant-manufacturing
and banking was consistent with the continuing development of
feudalism, though not with social stability, is buttressed with
three further arguments. First, towns did not necessarily free the

neighbouring countryside. Dobb cites the case of England where serfdom was eroded in the more remote north and west prior to many market-oriented areas in the south and east, and the case of the region around Paris which he believes saw trade and serfdom coexist during the late medieval period. A second argument adduced by Dobb is that feudal classes and their retainers were implicated in the market economy not only as consumers, but also in many instances as market-oriented producers in their own right. The introduction of a second serfdom on many landed estates in eastern Europe during the sixteenth and seventeenth centuries, for example, was largely stimulated by an increasing demand for arable products on European markets. While Wallerstein (1974) has recently interpreted this as a form of integration into the capitalist world system, Dobb's earlier argument was that it represented a degree of agrarian commercialism constrained with a framework of feudal property rights.

A third argument advanced by Dobb is that the new 'mercantile bourgeoisie' which grew up alongside such feudal elements was remarkably quick to compromise with feudalism, either by inter-marrying with noble families to upgrade social status, or by entering into political coalition with them. In this way Dobb combines a sense of the significant if limited dynamic in feudalism with the containment of the late medieval market economy within what he regards as an essentially agrarian feudal mode of production based on serfdom.

Dobb does not entirely dispense with the town in his explanation of transition, since he agrees that many serfs fled from rural exploitation and conflict to the urban setting. This process was however symptomatic of crisis within feudalism between the increasingly oppressive demands of lords for revenue and the productivity limitations imposed by serfdom, rather than a means of resolving feudal instability. While Abrams points to a certain ambiguity in Dobb as to the possibility of cities acting as autonomous *sui generis* entities, there is in general no special place for towns as such within the underlying thrust of his discussion. Dobb opts rather for an emphasis on certain agrarian origins of capitalism, forms of rural conflict between lords and serfs, and the subsequent differentiation of a free peasantry into capitalist farmers and wage labourers. The model is essentially based on the English experience.

Dobb's argument was challenged by Sweezy in a number of respects. For Sweezy, late medieval mercantile cities were not merely autonomous from feudalism but external to its underlying logic. This 'externality' stemmed, in Sweezy's view, from the function of cities as 'centres and breeders of the exchange economy' in contrast with what he took to be the self-sufficiency of the natural economy characteristic of feudalism. Like Pirenne before him, Sweezy organized his answer to the problem of transition to capitalism around the dynamic process that undermined the pre-existing system of production for use, and feudal servility. While Sweezy agreed that the late medieval cities did not as yet constitute capitalism, he none the less viewed them as dynamic components of a process of transition whereby change diffused outward from city to countryside. Sweezy's emphasis on urban-centred trade as the main solvent of feudalism has been likened by Brenner to a version of neo-Smithian Marxism involving a market-led explanation of transition.

Resolution of the conflict between Dobb and Sweezy is not simply a matter of further empirical exploration of the questions they debated on a rather slender data basis. This is because somewhat different conceptions of feudalism and capitalism are at stake. Dobb's somewhat naive methodological premise that debates about the nature of capitalism could be resolved by simple empirical inquiry (Dobb, 1963, p. 3) fails to take account of the differing intellectual purposes and research programmes that underly conceptual frameworks. Further assessment of the function and utility of differing conceptions of capitalism may be pursued elsewhere (see especially Holton, 1981, 1985). For present purposes, the main difficulty with Sweezy's position is that he failed to bring forward convincing evidence in favour of a discernible contrast between the developmental dynamic of urban institutions based on production for exchange and the supposedly conservative impact of rural institutions dependent on servility and production for use. In a sense, he took Pirenne's historical researches for granted. The net effect, however unintended, was to associate capitalism in a highly indiscriminate fashion with relationships of production for exchange that might be found as prominently among oriental traders in many parts of Asia or among the mercantile communities of the ancient Mediterranean, as in late medieval Europe. Dobb's conception of capitalism based on the commodification of labour power linked with expansive processes of capital accumulation is more serviceable because it posits a contingent relationship between production for exchange, the underlying character of the social structure, and the role of town and countryside in economic activity.

The thrust of empirical research since the initial exchange between Dobb and Sweezy has been to bring into question the notion that late medieval cities functioned as discrete and autonomous social milieux distinct from feudalism. Unless feudalism is defined in a highly technical manner in terms of dependent tenures held in return for military service, or in strictly spatial terms as an essentially rural order, there seems to be very little warrant for regarding distinctions between town and country either as coterminous with the distinction between capitalism and feudalism or with the notion of progressive and backward social spaces. The challenge this poses to urbanist theories of transition has several elements.

In the first place, considerable evidence has been assembled to challenge Pirenne's assertion that the origins of medieval towns involved mercantile settlement around older fortifications or ecclesiastical settlements, yet set apart from them by merchants' exclusive pursuit of trade. This theory, as we have seen, analysed medieval urban development in terms of the increasing political and juridical dominance of such autonomous groups whether achieved by usurpation or by a more gradualist process of negotiation. Hibbert (1953) by contrast showed that the origins of many substantial medieval towns depended, not on new men of an exclusively mercantile background, but on the initiative of nobles and aristocratic landowners. Such groups were involved in both late medieval Italy, about which Pirenne said comparatively little, and in many parts of northern Europe, in the development of urban self-government and in the promotion of economic activity. All this is not to deny the existence of periodic conflicts of jurisdiction and political authority, especially between larger feudal overlords and new urban communes. But

it is to deny the proposition that the urban centres of medieval
Europe were constituted in a manner thoroughly distinct from
and antipathetic to the feudal, landed or traditionalistic
environment.

Hibbert's analysis of urban origins has been consolidated in
more recent work. In the case of England, Hilton has demonstrated the importance of feudal landlords, whether lay or
ecclesiastical in the formation of new boroughs or towns in the
late medieval period. This included the recruitment of settlers,
the guarantee of local rights to hold markets, and in many cases
the offer of *burgage* tenure, that is, urban land held in uncon-
ditional ownership free from feudal controls. The aim here was
in large measure the extension of revenue raising activities
through the encouragement of economic activity subject to seigneurial exaction by landowners. Whereas Weber interpreted
burgage tenure within the new urban milieu as a manifestation of
urban autonomy from feudalism, Hilton shows the two to be
integrally related – at least at the outset.

Dollinger's (1970) study of the Hanseatic League – an association of north German cities such as Lübeck, Hamburg and
Bremen for the purposes of urban trading expansion – also
demonstrates the key role played by lords in urbanizing Germany at least in the origin of new settlements as self-governing
communities. Lübeck, which played an important part in Hanseatic trade between Russia and the Baltic, on the one hand, and
Western European centres like Bruges and London, on the other,
was originally founded in the twelfth century by Adolf, count of
Holstein, a vassal of the Duke of Saxony. The aim was to help
populate the German lands, to establish trading posts from
which profits might be made and to help Christianize the pagan
Slavs. The Knights of the Teutonic Order who settled much of
north German territory east of the Elbe within the Hanseatic
orbit, including urban centres like Danzig, also reflect a feudal
element in late medieval urban origins. Many dozens of German
towns, with their own communal constitutions were successfully
developed from origins such as this, though urban population
levels did not reach Flemish or Italian levels until the sixteenth
century.

German urban development was further characterized by the

appearance of 'free' imperial cities. These were 'protected' – not always effectively – by the political and military resources of the Holy Roman Empire. In cases such as Lübeck, imperial authority wrested jurisdiction away from local feudal controls. Imperial cities were in general far freer from feudal jurisdiction than their counterparts elsewhere. Even so, the periodic political feebleness of the Empire, especially in northern Germany, meant that feudal controls might be effectively reasserted since, as Dollinger points out, nearly all Hanseatic towns remained within the jurisdiction of lay or ecclesiastical authority and were hence liable to its reassertion.

What is more important then is how far the 'feudal' or 'seigneurial' *origins* of many significant mercantile cities were relevant to their evolution and longer-term dynamic. While theories of sharp discontinuity between feudalism and urban mercantile settlement are quite clearly untenable, it has still been argued that this feudal element receded in importance in the face of an increasingly modern market-oriented urban social structure. Weber cites the withdrawal of many Italian nobles from cities to rural estates in support of this argument. More importantly, his emphasis on the urban commune as a sworn association of individuals in contrast with ascriptively-structured patrimonial institutions is seen as a vital forerunner of rational-legal authority. This was at the very least conducive to, if not directly indicative of, the presence of capitalism. A stronger line of argument has been developed by George Unwin (1927), the English economic historian. He contrasts the militaristic ethos of feudalism with the voluntaristic character of medieval guilds in both their religious and economic activities. There is a direct link, in Unwin's view, between the guilds as autonomous organizations of individual economic actors, and the economic voluntarism of nineteenth century capitalism.

A Shift of attention from the origins and initial settlement to the continuing developmental significance of late medieval cities raises at least three sets of questions. How much autonomy from 'feudal' or 'seigneurial' structures had such cities come to possess by around 1300? Which institutions and practices expressed this autonomy? What if any developmental significance did such autonomy entail for the transition to capitalism? Such questions require a basic distinction to be made between the north Italian cities and those of the remainder of Western Europe north of the Alps.

In the Italian situation, we are dealing with city-states, responsible for their economic and political well-being in its entirety. Here urban centres were linked to a surrounding food and rent-producing rural hinterland of agricultural regions and small towns under the jurisdiction of the city. This city-state structure to some degree reflects the ancient origins of medieval Italian urbanism, from which the institution of the city-state derives. One important feature of this legacy was the continuing practice of rural landowners living in cities, as they had done in the ancient world (Bloch, 1961, p. 299). In this milieu urban/rural distinctions in the social structure and especially within the structure of political authority are less apposite than elsewhere. For landed nobles, especially those too small to have territorial ambitions over large regions, there was little cultural barrier to involvement on a continuing basis in urban activity. Within the economically expansive Italian cities it is not surprising therefore to find that landowners of noble or feudal origins worked alongside and intermingled with merchants and successful artisans, eventually fusing into a patrician elite. What is less appreciated is that the ethos of this elite involved a strong measure of feudal or traditionalistic status preoccupations. Over the long-term it was the successful merchants, bankers and manufacturers who were assimilated into this 'quasi-feudal' status structure, rather than the landed-aristocratic elements who were obliged to accept a new bourgeois world-view based on liberal-democratic individualism and business as a vocation.

The growing fusion and class morale of the Italian patricians – composed of an increasingly undifferentiated set of prominent merchant aristocrats – is reflected in the successful resistance to attempts to widen the basis of urban citizenship by including larger sections of the *popolo* within republican constitutions. In spite of social unrest and political mobilization, the situation after 1300 became increasingly oligarchical in the defence of the privileges of the wealthy. While Anderson (1974b, p. 150) cites Waley (1969) in support of the notion that the north Italian city-states allowed around one third of the citizenry to hold communal office in any one year, Martines (1983) reminds us that the percentage of the population enfranchised as citizens was usually a good deal less than 10 per cent, and sometimes as low as 2 per cent, as in fifteenth century Venice.

Meanwhile the aristocratic ethos of the city-states was manifested in an increasing shift from active entrepreneurial to a passive rentier outlook. This was associated with a process, referred to by Hale, the historian of Renaissance Florence, as 're-feudalization' which reached its peak in the fifteenth and sixteenth centuries. This was characterized by an emphasis on 'country villas, chivalrous poems, tournaments and an interest in genealogy', suggesting 'the attractiveness to wealthy merchants and bankers of an exclusiveness based on blood rather than effort' (Hale, 1979, p. 81). Such evidence testifies to the difficulty of distinguishing the culture of the ostensibly bourgeois city from the ostensibly feudal countryside. This point has been emphasized on a more general level by Heers (1977) in his emphasis on the importance of family clans in late medieval cities, especially those in Italy, Thus 'the great families of the urban aristocracy nearly always claimed rural origins and noble descent, looking to particular fiefs in particular villages . . . social structures in cities perpetuted those of the fiefs, for clans remained as powerful as before . . . the family clans of the towns mirrored those of the countryside' (ibid., pp. 248–9).

While the attribution of bourgeois individualism, on the model of Burckhardt's celebrated interpretation of the Renaissance (Burckhardt, 1929), is clearly inadequate, it seems equally problematic to describe such a dynamic society as that of northern Italy as feudal, where this term implies a militaristic ethos, or a pre-modern landed economy founded on servile labour. For set against the undoubted shift from economic to status preoccupations in the region after 1300 must be placed the many innovations in social life pioneered in cities like Florence and Venice. In response to the massive expansion of international commerce, transnational banking, merchant-sponsored craft production and the problem of securing urban economic and political stability a number of vital innovations emerged. These included double-entry book-keeping, the separation of business from personal accounts and the bill of exchange. New fiscal devices designed to protect and enlarge the economic and political strength of the city-state included the consolidation and funding of the public debt (Martines, 1983).

It is doubtful whether terms like 'feudal' or 'capitalist' with their respective evolutionary connotations of 'backward' and 'progressive' are suitable to the overall characterization of the complex mixture of forward and backward looking elements in northern Italian society at this time. What is perhaps more important is the estimation of the developmental significance of this experience. Two points stand out here. The first is that oligarchic government, guild restrictionism and an aristocratic quasi-feudal culture did not prevent a significant expansion of the north Italian economy and the emergence of important innovations, whose impact on the later history of European capitalism was very important in such spheres as capital accounting and the fiscal consolidation of the modern state. This indicates that significant advances towards capitalism do not necessarily depend on the presence of a new type of economic or political actor committed to a modern type of liberal-democratic individualism.

The second point of significance is that the Italian city-states, however innovatory, did not secure a successful and pioneering transition to capitalism, but fell back in terms of their economic leadership. Analysis of the reasons for this is a complex multi-faceted problem (see especially Cipolla, 1952, Aymard, 1982). There is considerable plausability none the less in the view that certain features of the city-state structure were unconducive to a final breakthrough to capitalism. First, the city-state was not a sufficiently large or powerful enough unit to maintain the political integrity of urban territory. The nation-state was to have far greater advantages both in terms of the scale of resources it could mobilize and, in an epoch of improved artillery, its lack of vulnerability to new methods of warfare which made city walls ineffective as defences. This was to be demonstrated in and after 1494 in the successful invasion by the French armies of many parts of northern Italy. Secondly the backward-looking cultural elements in the Italian fusion of aristocracy and wealth were more conducive to rentier activity than to entrepreneurship. At the very least this indicates that the presence of free urban labour, contingent on the abolition of serfdom, is not in itself a sufficient condition of transition to capitalism. Where restrictions on market development continue, whether due to the continuation of a largely self-sufficient free peasant hinterland, or to the dominance of luxury trades, it would not be attractive to deploy such free labour in larger-scale, more productive economic units.

The place of northern cities in the late medieval social structure contrasts to a certain extent with the Italian model. Between 1100 and 1400 a number of important mercantile and merchant-manufacturing cities emerged in this region, more especially in Flanders and the German lands. The highly urbanized Flemish region saw the growth of cities like Ghent, an important centre of cloth-making whose population reached around 60,000 by the late 1350s, and Bruges, a centre of the carrying trade as well as cloth production with 40,000 inhabitants (Nicholas, 1976, p. 24). Yet in spite of certain demographic and economic similarities, Flanders developed in a significantly different manner to the north Italian region.

In the first place, Flanders lacked the ancient Mediterranean tradition whereby the landed or feudal nobility resided in large part in the cities and participated in urban life. Although there is some evidence to suggest that Pirenne underestimated the extent to which feudal groups were responsible for the original settlement of towns like Dinant and Arras (Hibbert, 1953, pp. 99–100), it appears that in the longer term the Flanders region did develop a stronger sense of social division between urban-centred merchants and artisans, on the one side, and feudal landowners on the other. Nicholas (1968, p. 49) demonstrates that the Flemish nobility participated little in urban life, except as hired mercenaries of the great towns during the French Wars. For reasons that are not entirely clear, the Flemish nobility was by the end of the thirteenth century both economically and politically weak, such that 'the absolute independence of the town magistrates within the wall . . . except for a few token functions remaining to the capital officials and local lords, is indisputable' (ibid., p. 461).

A second important difference between Flanders and northern Italy is that the Flemish cities did not attempt to become city-states. Rather than incorporating town and country-side in a significantly sized territorial unit through the unifying agency of a patrician elite of interdependent landed and mercantile backgrounds, the smaller Flemish cities tended to restrict their jurisdiction to the town and its immediate environment. This left much of the rural social structure intact, except for rural-based industries close to the city which urban merchant-manufacturers sought to destroy.

Anderson (1974b) has pointed out that this type of city rather than the city-state is more widely characteristic of northern European towns. It is to be found in Germany as well as Flanders, both in the northern Hanseatic cities, urban settlements along the Rhine, and in south German cities involved in trade, manufacture and mining. Since the category 'city' is very far from homogenous, it is important to emphasize that the vast majority of German cities of the late Middle Ages had populations of less than 3,000 and were largely involved in local rather than long-distance trade, in satisfying local demand rather than specialist production and wholesale trade for distant markets. None the less, the larger cities, mostly under imperial protection, were able to grow to the size of the Flemish if not the larger Italian cities by 1500. The most important were Cologne, dominating the Rhine trade (nearly 40,000 inhabitants), Augsburg, a metal-working, banking and trading centre (50,000 inhabitants) and Nuremburg, another metal-working centre (30,000 inhabitants). Each, like their Flemish counterparts, had developed policies of political and juridical autonomy in support of urban wealth and privilege. While Dollinger (1970) has shown that the north German Hanseatic cities founded by feudal lords continued to ape feudal-aristocratic culture in their enthusiasm for epic and courtly poetry, their promotion of jousts and tourneys celebrating heroes such as Roland and Gunther, and their dependence on feudal patronage for the establishment of universities (pp. 264–6), the ethos of south and west German cities appears somewhat different. Here the model of the economically dynamic free imperial city, sharply differentiated behind its wall from the feudal or aristocratic countryside and possessed of a self-conscious self-governing *Bürgertum* appears to provide the origin of the lower Franconian proverb 'town air makes free'. What kind of freedom this constituted, and whether such 'freedom' was in any sense decisive for, or conducive to, the transition to capitalism, is more difficult to determine.

As with northern Italy, the case for any direct relationship between German or Flemish cities and successful transition to capitalism is difficult to make, since neither region played a prominent part at the forefront of socio-economic transformation until the nineteenth century industrialization and national consolidation of Germany and Belgium. It is none the less true that many late medieval Flemish and German cities saw considerable extensions of market-oriented economic activity, involvement in an increasing range of international markets, and, especially in the German case, a remarkable series of technological advances. Between 1450 and 1520, these included printing, ore-refining, smelting, ordnance manufacture and clock-making (Hobsbawm, 1965, pp. 17–18). Such developments, alongside the accounting, banking and fiscal innovations of the Italian city-states, were significant, though not in the main decisively important additions to the repertoire of innovations drawn on in later phases of transition to capitalism.

While it is important to bear in mind the distinction between the Italian fusion of feudal and mercantile elites, and the greater element of contrast between the two in many urban milieux north of the Alps, the distinction from a developmental viewpoint is one of degree not of kind. First, the political and juridical autonomy of the northern urban communes of the period 1100–1500 was rarely absolute but contingent on the political orientation and military strength of surrounding jurisdictions. These involved the parcellized sovereignties involved in the classic feudal institutions of fiefdom and vassalage. This parcellization process could be extended to give privileged status to the city as a corporation, and the rather special case of imperial jurisdiction which effectively offered privileges of a similar kind but unmediated through historic landed tenures.

In addition, surrounding jurisdictions increasingly took the form of nation-states built upon the centralization of authority and certain kinds of legal competence that had grown around what had previously been the personal patrimony of monarchs. In the case of thirteenth and fourteenth century England, where late medieval royal authority became more centralized than in most parts of continental Europe, urban communes developed from royal charters rather than seigneurial recognition. The achievement of urban autonomy by the growing mercantile and rentier classes of London via this route has been traced by Williams (1963). The securing of urban autonomy by royal charter was also important in northern France where central royal authority was increasing. In the case of late medieval Paris – whose fourteenth century population had reached 200,000, far in excess of London – the predominant urban functions of royal capital and centre of administration and learning produced a far weaker degree of autonomy (Diefendorf, 1983) than was achieved in the more diversified mercantile and administrative capital of late medieval London.

In analysing the general character of late medieval autonomy there are two traps into which interpretations may fall. The first is to visualize juridically autonomous cities as effective puppets of feudal or regalian authority. Urban autonomy in such fields as market control, economic protection and separate legal jurisdiction was real, even if conditional. This is more easy to appreciate if Western urban autonomy is compared with the far more precarious position of urban merchants in civilizations such as pre-modern China where centralized bureaucratic control militated against the formation of corporate urban jurisdictional autonomy. (For further elaboration of this point see Chapter 5.)

The second trap is to invest Western urban autonomy with an over-inflated sense of the precocious emergence of economic individualism and liberal-democratic freedom. Late medieval cities were not 'islands of capitalism in a sea of feudalism'. Essentially urban autonomy was a form of privilege, granted by a feudal or royal source of authority, which could be, and often was, reversed. They may be seen as examples of the more general evolution of a post-manorial polity – the northern European *Standestaat*, or polity of estates. Unlike the Italian city-states who sought to retain state-like sovereignty, Europe's late medieval towns became integrated as distinct corporate bodies into a system of government also involving kings and extra-urban feudal lords.

Merrington (1975) has struggled to find the words by which to avoid these two pitfalls, emerging with the notion of 'internal externality'. By this means he finds a way round the interminable conundrum which Marxists must face as to whether cities are internal or external to feudalism. They are both, meaning that urban autonomy is patterned on a feudal model, but has a developmental significance leading toward capitalism. This helpful formulation is consistent with Istvan Rev's (1984) argument that it is not 'urban air' that makes 'free', but 'privilege'. In other words any developmental dynamic connected with late medieval cities is to be connected not with some early breakthrough to modern liberal-democratic pluralism, but with the granting of corporate feudal privileges to cities. Pirenne certainly recognized this in as much as he warned against assimilating the late medieval city in any simplistic manner into modern notions of individual freedom. His theory of mercantile settlement none the less obscured the alternative possibility that late medieval cities operated very much as 'collective seigneurs', an idea already present within nineteenth century French historiography and recently revived by Merrington (1975).

If the incorporation of late medieval cities within existing structures of authority cannot any longer be doubted, it remains to be seen exactly what kind of milieux existing within the city, and what developmental dynamic arose therefrom. The first point to emphasize here is that late medieval cities were generally undemocratic, involving vast inequalities in both wealth and political power. In Flanders, the percentage of *poorters* – the legal corporation of urban landowners who constituted the commune – within the total population was larger than in Italy, but still limited to around 10–12 per cent (Nicholas, 1976, p. 16). Handfuls of patrician families were to dominate the city government in many German and English cities in the late medieval and early modern period (Braudel, 1982, pp. 466–70). Over time a number of guilds, usually involving the wealthier merchants or entrepreneurial associations, gained formal rights of participation in urban government. Very few late medieval cities saw government dominated by guilds as such in part because the privileged status concerns of leading families, and those who aspired to join them, overrode any primary identification as an economic actor.

The containment of late medieval political participation within narrow privileged circles reflects the continuing predominance of ascriptive ties of status over any more universalistic conception of citizen. If urban air was 'free', this freedom neither comprised modern egalitarian citizenship rights, nor absolute individual property rights. Not only were all citizens male, but also in many cases males heads of a narrow range of families. In a number of cities, a place in the citizen body was either hereditary – deriving from the original families of the commune – or the outcome of a somewhat ad hoc collection of criteria including the accumulation of wealth, residence qualification, or successful completion of an apprenticeship. In the imperial city of Cologne in the fourteenth century it was necessary to be male, a Catholic, a successful guild member and a resident (Diefendorf, 1980, p. 24). All this of course represents a shift away from strictly feudal associational ties of vassalage dependent on a hierarchy of mutual obligations within an aristocratic class. Yet it is hard to recognize within it those ideal types of achievement by merit, or liberal-democratic individualism based on freely consenting equals, characteristic of what is usually taken to be a modern world-view consistent with capitalism.

Recent protagonist of the Weberian ideal-typical view of the Western city, such as Poggi (1983), have recognized a continuing ascriptive element in the late medieval urban context. The urban citizenry is regarded as an estate rather than a class – a status-conscious *Bürgertum*, rather than bourgeoisie. Yet for all this the linking of the burgher estate with the capitalist bourgeoisie of the nineteenth century as part of an over-arching history of occidental urbanism contains the danger of reading back 'modern' anticipations or forerunners into the past. Although Poggi seeks to avoid the grosser forms of anachronistic imputation involved in the familiar teleological interpretation of Western history where the middle class is somehow always on the rise, there remains an exaggerated sense of unity and continuity in his underlying urbanist world-view. Thus,

No matter how much they differ in other terms, the priests and theologians, the lawyers, the journalists, the politicians, the university professors, the functionaries of public and private bureaucracies, the artists and musicians, the stock jobbers and the bankers, who people Weber's pages, often [sic!] have in common with one another, and with the entrepreneurs, their membership in one larger social entity – the Western Bürger-tum. (Poggi, 1983, p. 112)

We are left wondering how 'often' is often, and what are the other 'terms' by which such occupational groups may differ.

Recent contributions to the history of the concepts *Bürger,* *Bürgertum* and bourgeoisie suggest that the notion of an evolving European *Bürgertum* is incoherent as a unitary cultural phenomenon within the history of the West (see especially Riedel, 1975). Whatever may be said about the very real pride and self-consciousness of late medieval towns, or about the contrasts between Europe's distinctively urban corporations of burgesses, guildsmen and citizens and the weak or non-existent articulation of urban groups in the non-European world, the meaning of the term *Bürger* (and its other European equivalents) with the late medieval and early modern Europe is far more variable and far less consistent over time and space than has usually been realized. Having originated as a term describing those responsible for the defence and maintenance of a fortified place (burgh), it subsequently became defined in terms of five overlapping but not necessarily congruent criteria. These comprised:

1 A *juridical* criterion based on restrictive membership of the urban commune, which in turn gave access to office and communal privileges. At its strictest this involved the descendant families of the original free founders of the commune, but later widened to include
2 A *property* criterion founded on ownership of urban property, originally held as burgage tenure. While often coterminous with commune membership, property ownership did not necessarily entail active involvement in economic activity, being consistent with rentier status.
3 A *status* criterion founded on the distinction between nobles, clerics and burgers, defined as residents of towns generally engaged in trade and manufacture.
4 A *residence* criterion, essentially town dwellers as a whole,

that is, all those within the city walls or adjacent suburbs contrasted with what lay beyond.

5 An *occupational* criterion, involving the successful completion of a guild apprenticeship.

Such elements do not represent a unitary common core to the notion of 'burgher', but exist in quite varied, complex and often mutually inconsistent usages within the various urban settings of late medieval and early modern Europe. This is evident from close inspection and comparison of the following monographic and interpretative studies: Diefendorf, 1983, pp. xxiii–iv, Friedrichs, 1975, pp. 27–9, Riedel, 1975, pp. 672–723, Swart, 1975, pp. 46 ff, Walker, 1971, pp. 44–59, Zagorin, 1969, pp. 120–22.

At the level of the wider territorial unit within which individual cities were located further complexities arise. These apply to the *Standestaat* systems, whereby towns were intimately involved in wider structures of authority involving monarchical and feudal groups (Poggi, 1978). It has been pointed out by Riedel (1975) that such towns did not participate in such systems as clear cut representatives of a definable urban interest, but rather as representatives of all who were neither noble nor clerical, that is a 'Third Estate' of heterogenous composition. All this suggests the need for great care in using the notion of the Western *Bürgertum* as a discrete cultural product of late medieval society, and hence as an organizing framework for the analysis of transition to capitalism.

Aside from the problem of cultural coherence there remains the problem of historical continuity between *Bürgertum* and bourgeoisie. The case in favour of such continuity is not negligible in so far as late medieval cities took considerable steps forward both in the accumulation of urban mercantile capital and in the consolidation of more positive views of private involvements in economic life than had existed in the ancient Mediterranean world. Certain elements of modern rational-legal jurisdiction may also be detected in the fiscal rationalization of certain city-states. Having said all this, what remains is a strong impression of the privileged, restrictive, patriarchal, and status bound character of social life in this period. The possibility of continuities between this rather less modern characterization of the late medieval world and modern capitalism none the less remain, in so far as it can be shown that capitalism itself, at least in its seventeenth and eighteenth century phases of consolidation, was far from coterminous with the absence of privilege, economic restriction and patriarchy.

Much of the analysis of transition to capitalism has been formed in terms of what Bryan Turner has called the 'great divide' theory in which massive discontinuity is posed between capitalism and the feudal world that went before (Turner, 1981, p. 290). This assumption of discontinuity has fed into the transition debate, inviting the search for forerunners of which is taken to be modernity within a pre-modern setting. Within a Weberian framework, for example, many scholars have scoured late medieval cities for historical forerunners of those characteristics such as economic rationalization, primary commitment to secular economic goals and individual achievement, separation of family and workplace and bureaucratization, constitutive of modernity. One problem with this approach is that many of the decisive phases of early capitalist consolidation, as in Britain and nineteenth century Europe, combined sectors of innovation (for example, in technology, work organization and international trade) with sectors of continuity (for example, in business organization, family structure, valuation of community, high status accorded to landed wealth, personnel of government). Transition to capitalism (in terms of the commodification of labour power and the transformation of productive forces) occurred, at least in this phase, primarily through the family firm, with a continuing shift from entrepreneurial to rentier landed status on the part of new wealth, and within a governmental context dominated in large measure by those of landed origins. Hence it does not seem necessary to require that the origins of capitalist development depended in any fundamental way on a lessening of family or kinship ties in the conduct of business, on the acceptance of the entrepreneurial vocation as a permanent role, or upon a strong bourgeois presence in government. While the thrust of twentieth century Western society may indeed be towards further rationalization of this kind, such developments may not be entirely germane to discussions of the first phase of modern capitalist development. There may, in other words, be greater historical discontinuities between early and late phases in the development of modern capitalism (Turner, 1981; see also Parsons, 1971) than between feudalism and early modern capitalism.

A related problem concerns the liberal economic interpretation of capitalist development. This stresses the individualist *laissez-faire* or at least voluntaristic element in modern capitalism, thereby shifting inquiry into historical origins towards pre-modern forerunners of individualism, and the undermining of economic regulation. The modern idea that medieval guilds and the early modern absolutist state acted as obstacles to social change, derives from eighteenth-century liberal economists. An alternative possibility, however, is that the relationship between capitalist development and *laissez-faire* is a contingent rather than a necessary one. Polanyi (1977), for example, has argued that the so-called free market system is a historically exceptional and transitory form, characteristic of Britain in the mid to late nineteenth century, but not before or after and even less typical of continental Europe. It may then be misleading to demand that the origins and inner logic of the transition process may be located within some kind of precocious historical phase of individualism or lack of regulation.

Taken together these two re-evaluations of the nature of capitalism (or early capitalism) – the phenomenon whose emergence is to be explained – suggest fresh perspectives on the late medieval city. Rather than torturing the evidence to find forerunners of individualism in the sworn confraternities of the urban communes, or to sustain some unitary sense of the dynamic European *Bürgertum*, it seems more appropriate to ask how it was that certain socio-economic breakthroughs occurred within a context that remained, to modern eyes at least, uneasily poised between feudalism and capitalism, where quasi-modern elements appear in traditional guise, and traditionalism seems to bring forth dynamic consequences of an unintended kind.

One of the main areas of empirical inquiry posed by this theoretical re-evaluation centres on the economic restrictions constitutive of late medieval European cities. These included the protectionist policies of cities and city-states towards the monopolistic market and trading rights of their merchants and producers, the restriction on the production of rural competitors located outside the immediate urban sphere, guild regulation of the quality and scale of production, the protection of technical innovations from outsiders, and the restrictions placed on goods in transit from other areas. Were such controls so inhibitive of capitalist development as the conventional historiography implies?

Thrupp (1963), in her important general survey of the economic consequences of medieval guilds, has counselled caution with respect to the largely negative evaluation of conventional scholarship. She makes three main points. The first is that restriction on the scale of output had a far less damaging effect on productivity where goods were produced for buoyant export markets, as in northern Italy or Flanders, rather than exclusively local production. In the latter case relatively limited markets did little to encourage expansion and innovation, such that the lifting of output restrictions would have caused over-supply and dislocation. The rationale for limitations was therefore to protect the livelihood of local producers. In the former case, by contrast, expanding export markets could be satisfied within the framework of guild controls since they did not threaten to destabilize the local economy.

Next, Thrupp argues that the *de facto* operation of the late medieval economy was less rigid than evidence of *de jure* controls might indicate. Restrictions could and often were circumvented provided the incentive and will to do so was there in the first place. Where incentives were lacking, there was no economic rationale for erosion of restriction. Thrupp concludes that guild restrictions were in large measure a rational response to an economic environment in which mass markets were non-existent and the maximization of output and productivity were generally inappropriate. This point may be supplemented by Le Goff's (1972) argument, following Mickwitz (1936), that guild controls on entry into trades served as a kind of Malthusian regulation. The status of 'master', which implied the material capacity for family formation, and into which entry was limited, was distinguished from 'journeyman', paid by the day and seen as inconsistent with married status.

Since much of the restrictive element of guilds was either

rational, given prevailing economic conditions, or capable of evasion, it is difficult to regard them as fundamental obstacles to capitalist development. The most clear-cut examples of restriction impeding general economic development, if not the economic stability of individual towns, involves the control over innovation often to the point of extreme secrecy and hostility to outsiders. Postan cites the case of the Bologna silk industry where the invention of a silk-throwing machine was kept secret from 1272 until 1538 until discovered by the ruse of an Englishman (Postan, 1973). Similarly, the city of Nuremburg protected the new technology of mechanical wire-milling from competitors from 1415 until 1511 (von Stromer, 1981, p. 127).

The well-known evasion of guild controls by re-location of production outside city jurisdiction within rural villages and the countryside, often through the putting-out (or *Verlags*) system, is indicative of the fact that restrictions were not so tight as to be able to retard change. Since much of the initiative for such changes derived from urban merchant-manufacturers they clearly tend to support certain kinds of urbanist theory. At the same time the lack of concern shown by urbanist theory towards the possibility of agrarian origins of rural industry, and the evolution of continuing patterns of urban/rural interdependence, represent (see pp. 100 ff) a serious empirical weakness in the urbanist case.

It has often been pointed out that the urban basis of the successful transition to capitalism in the seventeenth and eighteenth centuries was located, not in the old medieval guild centres, but in newly emergent centres outside guild control. In the English case, for example, it is in Manchester, Birmingham and Sheffield rather than Coventry, Norwich or Exeter that the Industrial Revolution took root (Daunton, 1978). Where exactly this argument places London, by far the largest British city with its combination of guilds and unregulated production linked to local and inter-provincial trade, is not at all clear. More important, the reasons for the emergence of new industrial cities in this later period owe far more to the location of raw materials and sources of energy than they do to the intransigent restrictions of guild-controlled areas.

Since the history of modern capitalism is full of instances of corporate restriction and monopolistic regulation and protectionism, much of it sanctioned by the state, it is to be doubted whether restrictions on free market exchange *per se* are unconducive to capitalist development. What is clear, however, is that the particular forms of guild control which developed in the late medieval period and survived well into modern Western history were more compatible with an economy fractured by the sectional interests of small-scale corporate units than with a polycentric interdependent system of capitalist exchange seeking out the optimization of profit through the deployment of relatively mobile factors of production, labour included. Guilds may not have been fundamental obstructions but nor were they significant causal agents in the process of economic change.

Having said this it is important not to loose sight of the possibility that autonomous guild organizations represent a manifestation of a more general Western phenomenon, namely, a growing differentiation between economic and political organization. The fact that economic groups such as merchants and producers were able to organize in a way which was distinct from centralized state initiative and control may have a more diffuse significance for the history of the West in signifying the legitimacy of autonomous economic activity. This autonomy may be easier to perceive when occidental economic organizations are compared with the far more tightly controlled imperial-bureaucratic systems of ancient Mediterranean or of Asian societies. It is not, however, necessary to imbue this autonomy with the notion of a unitary bourgeois preserve in late medieval and early modern Western cultures.

Any general verdict on the connection between late medieval cities and feudalism, from the viewpoint of transition to capitalism, has to come to terms with the following considerations. First, the history of the late medieval city reveals a complex blend of dynamic and conservative elements. In consequence it is difficult to consign the city at this stage to either the 'feudal' or 'capitalist' conceptual pigeon-holes. Late medieval cities were neither islands of capitalism in a sea of feudalism, nor part of an unchanging feudal order that had seen no dynamic change since the early Middle Ages. While Marxists have tended to show little conceptual imagination in handling this lack of correspondence between the city/country divide and the capitalist/feudal dichotomy, Weberians have shown too much imagination in projecting an over-inflated evolutionary continuity between medieval *Bürgertum* and the modern bourgeoisie.

A second set of problems surround the predominantly evolutionary and teleological framework within which urbanist theory is set. This approaches the development of capitalism in terms of a strong sense of historical continuity, associated with various dynamic agents of change endogenous to European society. The history of the Occident is taken as possessing an inner logic and potential linked to the city as bearer of civilization. While Pirenne uses the metaphor of historical 'steps', with the late medieval city standing as it were on the first rung of the ascending ladder of capitalist development, Le Goff (1972) has spoken of late medieval cities passing the 'baton' to their successors, as if Western history were a relay race. The trouble is, of course, that history is not a ladder the purpose of which is to be successfully climbed, nor is it a relay race which some team must win. Even if we retain such metaphors as organizing frames for exploring possible continuities in long-run processes of social change, the only guarantee that anyone can successfully climb the ladder without falling off or that at least one team can avoid dropping the baton is an *ex post facto* one. To posit any necessary connection between late medieval cities and the subsequent transition to capitalism in such evolutionary terms imbues Western development with an unwarranted sense of historical necessity and continuity, thereby also exaggerating contrasts between the West and the world beyond. Such overtones of historical necessity are built into the very language of transition from feudalism to capitalism.

The more specific historical arguments against teleological interpretations linking the late medieval city with the transition to capitalism depend on notions of 'crisis' and discontinuity in history. Two major movements of social crisis significantly disrupting and transforming the history of both town and countryside within Europe occurred in the fourteenth century and again in the seventeenth century. These may be connected with the vulnerability of late medieval Europe, especially its cities, to problems of inadequate food supply and subsistence, particularly in the seventeenth century with the development of the nation-state. Between them, these crises and success or failure in resolving the problems posed by them go a long way towards solving a major riddle of European historical sociology, namely the hiatus between the urban autonomy and self-confidence of the late medieval period, and the emergence of an urban-centred capitalist bourgeoisie in the eighteenth century. For as Weber himself pointed out, the trajectory of urban development is characterized not by an ever-onward-and-upward extension of late medieval urban influence, but rather by its loss of autonomy and displacement from the forefront of change during the early modern period.

THE RELATIONSHIP BETWEEN CITY AND COUNTRYSIDE IN THE TRANSITION TO CAPITALISM

There can be little doubt that classical political economy and sociological thought prior to 1900 gave little warrant for serious analytical consideration of the countryside as an important locus of socio-economic innovation relevant to the transition to capitalism. This reflected a sense of social change as coterminous with the processes of urbanization and industrialization. The economy, political structure and cultural practices of urban society were sharply distinguished from those of landed society, as may be seen in the familiar oppositions of *Gemeinschaft/ Gesellschaft*, status/contract, and feudal/capitalist. The late nineteenth century notion of 'industrial revolution' (Toynbee, 1884) was further appropriated by the triumphant urban model, quickly reinforcing existing views that the transition to modern Western society was a thoroughly revolutionary process, dependent on industrial technology located in urban centres and deployed by an essentially dynamic bourgeois class.

If the sharp edges of such dichotomies have more recently been softened by confrontation with discordant empirical material, this has generally been organized around the proposition of the persistence of the 'traditional' within the 'modern'. With the exception of Barrington Moore (1966) and recent Marxist agrarian history in the tradition of Maurice Dobb, far less attention has been given to the possibility that the ostensibly 'traditional' landed society might itself be implicated in a direct manner as a causal influence on the constitution of modern society. Although the urbanist edifice has begun to crack, Marx's assumption that 'the bourgeoisie historically has played a most revolutionary part' (Marx and Engels, 1962, p. 36) remains the predominant interpretation of the class basis to the rise of Western capitalism.

While there may be serious problems in projecting an upward linear progression from the late medieval cities to the modern urban industrial environment, and from the medieval *Bürgertum* to the modern bourgeoisie, protagonists of the urbanist theory of transition to capitalism can still point to the revival of urban development after crisis and set-back in the fourteenth and fifteenth centuries. Although the north Italian cities experienced population stagnation or even decline for a century or so after 1300–50, the centre of gravity of Europe's economic and urban life can be seen shifting northward and westward in the following centuries. Much of this shift may be linked with the movement from Mediterranean to Atlantic centred trade. Between 1450 and 1600 Europe's urban development took off again with the expansion of intra-European trade in food and manufactured goods as well as trade with the Americas and Africa, as well as with Asia.

In Flanders, the port of Antwerp expanded in the late fifteenth and early sixteenth centuries to join the earlier Flemish urban centres as an important locus of intra-regional trade. In the longer term, however, it was the northern parts of the Low Countries which were to produce a more dramatic urban economic expansion. By the mid-seventeenth century, the newly independent United Provinces (centred on Holland) had produced an urban network of half a million people centred on the trading and banking functions of Amsterdam and the manufacturing activities of surrounding cities such as Leyden (Clark, 1976, p. 2 and Burke, 1974). In Amsterdam, as for other west coast ports such as Lisbon, Seville, Nantes, Bordeaux, Bristol and Liverpool, the population expanded and mercantile groups prospered in part with the secular expansion of commerce across the oceans. In Germany the centre of gravity swung northward with Hamburg displacing Augsburg and Nuremburg as the leading mercantile town alongside Cologne by the early seventeenth century (Dollinger, 1970, p. 355). Meanwhile some of the most dramatic processes of expansion occurred with the rise of capital cities. The population of Paris grew from 200,000 in the mid-fourteenth century, to reach almost 500,000 by 1700 (Wrigley, 1967, p. 44), while London, from far smaller late medieval origins, had reached a population of 317,000 by 1632 and 700,000 by 1700 (Braudel, 1973, p. 431). Scale is not of course everything and is certainly not coterminous with economic dynamism or social innovation. This is reflected in the expansion of the poverty-stricken south Italian capital of Naples whose population had grown to 400,000 by the mid-eighteenth century. There is none the less an underlying secular sense of the vitality of urban-centred Europe between 1500 and 1800 at precisely that moment when the critical phases of transition to capitalism are typically located.

The prominence of this expansive urban element in mercantile and manufacturing activity may certainly be taken as an indication of more general processes of economic growth. The regions with the highest rates of urbanity around 1700, such as England and Holland, may be regarded as leaders in early modern capitalist development in comparison with France whose degree of urbanity and economic performance up to the eighteenth century was less impressive. Yet the analytical problem remains as to whether transition at that time was essentially urban-stimulated – the countryside being revolutionized as it were from outside – or whether the urban revival was in part made possible either by largely autonomous agrarian change or by complex forms of urban-rural interdependence.

The case against a unilateral urbanist explanation of this process may be assembled from three analytically distinct, though empirically interconnected problems. These may be listed as follows:

1 The problem of agrarian primary accumulation and labour supply.
2 The neo-Malthusian problem of food supply in relation to urban population.
3 The problem of rural proto-industrialization.

Agrarian Primary Accumulation

The main argument here, deriving from Marx, but elaborated more recently by Dobb and his successors, locates the 'primary accumulation' process whereby peasant agriculture was undermined and labour power commodified within the European countryside. Dobb, for example, maintains that the economic and social crises created by the limitations of feudal property relations were resolved not so much through further urban-centred processes of economic expansion in the late medieval model, but through two alternative mechanisms. The first involved agrarian class conflict between lords and serfs, prompted by decline in feudal revenue and increased exploitation of labour. Where this was resolved in favour of serfs by the granting or securing of free (or freer) landed tenures, a peasantry of small independent producers was created. The second stage in the model involves the further differentiation of the peasantry into capitalist farmers and wage-labourers, through processes such as enclosure of common land and centralization of holdings. Where these processes are combined (and here the model rests on fourteenth and fifteenth century England) both the 'feudal' and 'peasant' constraints on capitalist development are eroded. The principal mechanism at work here is the undermining of constraints on labour mobility allowing commodification of labour, and widening of the basis of economic activity from mercantile activity to an unhindered process of capital accumulation. Without such changes in the social relations of agrarian production, the urban economic base of European society would have been restricted to mercantile and rentier activity consistent with 'feudalism'.

The importance of this line of argument is twofold. First, it suggests that the mercantile and merchant-manufacturing basis of the late medieval economy was too restricted to bring about the social changes necessary to produce the transition to a modern capitalist economy. The restrictions on labour mobility posed by perpetuation of serfdom or peasant agriculture were not, of course, always inconsistent with a certain commercialization of agriculture. The historic difficulties in securing a more fundamental development beyond agricultural commercialization towards a more thorough-going industrial capitalist economy – whether on the serf-based manorial economies in eastern Europe or the peasant-based agriculture of much of France – are indicative of the need for changes in the social relations of production in the countryside *prior* to the expansion of industrial 'productive forces' characteristic of the modern capitalist epoch. What Dobb leaves unclear is the nature of the social agents involved in agrarian transformation, and the relative importance of labour supply compared with other potential contributions from the agrarian sector to the development of urban-industrial capitalism.

The question of agency and rationale behind changes in agrarian social relations, including the demise of serfdom and the erosion of the communal rights of peasants, has prompted wide debate. Part of this concerns the significance of urban landed investment. While the phenomena itself was widespread in early modern Europe, what is less clear is the extent to which the buying up of landed estates – often by successful merchants – was a function of desires to maximize profits through extension of the provenance of 'capitalism' from city to countryside. Economic motives for estate purchase certainly existed, though they often involved desires for a safe investment rather than an entrepreneurially inspired capital switch (Nicholas, 1968, 1971, Hoffman 1977, pp. 293–4). Meanwhile considerations of enhanced status and political influence contingent on membership of landed society very often loomed large (Nicholas, 1971, Thrupp, 1948, Herlihy, 1967, Grassby, 1970).

Beyond this there exists considerable evidence of social agents within landed society, and from an essentially rural background, being involved in processes of agrarian change. Much debate here centres on the relative importance of initiatives by large landowners *vis-à-vis* smaller producers, including tenant farmers and the larger peasantry (Brenner, 1982, Croot and Parker, 1978). Paucity of data makes this difficult to resolve. One tentative conclusion which may be drawn is that the role of smaller farmers was likely to be greater in technical changes such as, improved crop rotations and animal husbandry, than in the large and expensive organizational changes often involved in enclosure and the full economic exploitation of estates.

A second important aspect of Dobb's argument is the integration of social conflict and class struggle into the model of capitalist development. This theme addresses the widespread development of peasant unrest, which formed a prominent component of the fourteenth century crisis in European social development, reflected in the English peasant revolt of 1341 and the French *jacqueries* of the 1370s and 1380s. Within this perspective, the question of changing agrarian social relations is not reduced to one of landlord attitudes towards improvement and economic rationality versus status, but rather located within a structural conflict between lords and serfs over control of the economic surplus, and disposition of serf labour. Brenner (1976, 1977) has extended Dobb's argument here to assert rural class mobilization as an autonomous feature of late medieval and early modern history. His claim that success or failure in challenges to landlord domination may be linked to variations in peasant community structure between the European regions (stronger in the west, weaker in the east) has not, however, stood up all that well to subsequent criticism (Wünder, 1978).

A rather more provocative argument suggested by Hilton (1973), in his study of the English Peasant Revolt, is that modern notions of individual economic sovereignty and economic individualism may derive in large measure from peasant struggles to free themselves from the feudal and seigneurial controls of landowners. For Hilton, the concept of the free man owing no obligation, not even deference, is seen as 'one of the most important if intangible legacies of medieval peasants to the modern world' (1973, p. 235). Rural air, so to speak, can make free! This possibility points to what might be seen as a 'Germanic' theory of capitalist emergence founded on agrarian individualism, in contrast to the 'classical' or 'Romanist' urban-centred theories. Macfarlane (1978) in his recent work on English individualism has raised just this possibility, going back to Tacitus' comments on the agrarian practices of the Germanic tribes in the first century AD as a somewhat speculative indicator of a long-run continuity in the agrarian individualist tradition.

Macfarlane's work is important in drawing attention to the functioning of markets for land and commodities in late medieval England. It is doubtful, however, whether the evidence he presents amounts to convincing proof that 'the majority of ordinary people in England from at least the thirteenth century were rampant individualists' (ibid., p. 163) or that 'England was as capitalist in 1250 as it was in 1550 or 1750' (ibid., p. 195). One of the main problems with this argument is that little discussion is provided of the relationship between ostensibly 'individualistic' market activities and the wider social and cultural setting. Phenomena like serfdom, landlord–peasant relations involving matters like enclosures and the common field system are not investigated in sufficient depth for the constraints they placed on individualism. As Holton (1985, p. 45) points out, Macfarlane's method 'represents a very simplistic version of the classic Anglo-Saxon theories of immanent capitalistic emergence, whereby market economy is seen as entailing market society'. While Macfarlane has certainly helped to demolish simplistic theories of static peasant idiocy for the late medieval period he has not said the final word on the complex process of agrarian capitalist development.

Aside from the question of the historical origins of agrarian individualism, there remains the problem of the relative importance of labour supply mechanisms, as against other linkages between the landed and urban sectors. A good deal of recent economic history, following Chambers (1953), has sought to modify the cataclysmic view of enclosure and industrial revolution envisaged by Marx. The argument here, based essentially on England, is that the transformation of agrarian social relations involved in the enclosure of common land – in the sixteenth and eighteenth centuries – did not force vast numbers to flock to the cities as potential wage workers. While creating distress and dislocation the impact of enclosures was generally far less dramatic since agrarian employment continued to rise up to the mid-nineteenth century. The most that can be claimed is that potential for labour mobility was eased by changes in property relations involved in the remarkable demise of the English peasantry between the fourteenth and eighteenth centuries.

The neo-Malthusian problem of food supply
Problems of feeding rather than simply supplying labour to growing cities are a prominent thread in the strongly neo-Malthusian interpretation of the barriers to successful transition

to capitalism advanced by Postan (1972, 1973) and Le Roy Ladurie (1969, 1974) and taken into Marxist discourse by Anderson (1974a). The essence of this argument is that constraints on agrarian productivity must set limits to the capacity of cities to grow, and the capacity of any society to shift resources from food production to industrial production. This theoretical premise is closely linked to the long-run rhythms of the European economy prior to the consolidation of modern capitalism. Such rhythms comprise phases of population expansion, extension of cultivated land, and urban growth checked by phases of crisis where population outstrips available land and food supply leading to subsistence crises and contraction. One such phase of expansion is to be seen in the tenth to the thirteenth centuries, to be followed by collapse in the fourteenth century. This crisis involved class conflict, but this was the product of more fundamental structural imbalance between food supply and population within existing feudal constraints (Anderson, 1974a). The advent of the fourteenth century Black Death which decreased population levels by one third in some regions occurred, therefore, in a period of pre-existing crisis where population levels had declined from their late thirteenth century peak and famine had already set in (Postan, 1950).

This framework is important because it reminds us that the two phases of urban expansion in the late medieval and early modern periods occurred at a time when cities were still intensely vulnerable to fluctuations and uncertainties in food supply. To cite statistics of urban growth from one period to the next without due recognition of this vulnerability is to attribute a far greater degree of economic autonomy from the countryside to cities and urban life than is warranted. Food riots for example continued to be a major form of urban social unrest in Europe up to the early nineteenth century (Rudé, 1964). In the seventeenth century in particular, another profound demographic crisis was experienced in most regions of Europe, but particularly seriously in Spain, eastern France and Germany. Although epidemic disease and famine was widespread, two areas where the impact of the demographic crisis was least severe were Holland, which registered an increase in population, and England.

There is an important contrast at this time between England

and Holland, both of which managed either to grow or import most of their food needs and to expand their commerce and manufacturing, and certain of the previous leading sectors of the European economy such as the north Italian city-states, the Hanseatic towns, and many of the German cities. It was at this time, for example, that Italy was transformed from a leading urban-industrial centre to a declining 'typically backward peasant area' (Hobsbawm, 1965, p. 9). While there are many specific factors to be taken into account in explaining such contrasts between regions, one general thread that stands out is the importance of prior innovations in the rural sector in enabling regions to cope relatively successfully with European crisis. At the time of the fourteenth century, few such changes in the form of capitalist organization of farming and new more productive techniques were present in sufficient numbers to offset crisis. By the seventeenth century, England and Holland had made considerable advances in this sector and were hence better able to meet general conditions of economic downturn compared with the other European regions.

What the neo-Malthusian model does not adequately supply is an explanation of how and why certain regions may break out of the population–food supply trap. Le Roy Ladurie, for example, speaks of a certain 'unlinear drift in the direction of agrarian capitalism' within the 'homeostatic system' with its built-in mechanism of self-correction (1978b, p. 56). This is not, however, specified very clearly. He does none the less reject the 'sort of Augustinian, Calvinist or Jansenist view of history', which he associates with Brenner (1976, 1977) whereby 'the peasant has to be overwhelmed [and] expropriated by the action of lords who themselves become agents of the capitalist triumph' (Le Roy Ladurie, 1978, p. 59). This landlord-sponsored agrarian capitalism from above, indicative perhaps of the English mode of transition, under-estimates the capacity of the peasant family economy for change.

Any general assessment of the capacity of England and Holland to withstand the seventeenth century crisis so as to secure a further impressive consolidation of capitalist development must take into account the interdependence of rural and urban sources of innovation. On the English side, agrarian output was increased in part through landlord-sponsored 'improvement'. This should not necessarily be taken to mean either an intentional commitment to economic rationality or a sympathetic concern for the welfare of rural producers. Whatever the aims of individual landlords, the pressure to increase estate revenue had the effect of undermining hereditary and fixed tenures and creating a more vulnerable group of tenant farmers operating on a leasehold basis, effectively as capitalist farmers. Further sources of innovation usually from direct producers were evident in such areas as convertible husbandry and stock improvement (Croot and Parker, 1978). In the process, agricultural specialization by region became more prominent. Although such processes may be linked to a general population expansion in the sixteenth century, involving expansion of rural as well as urban demand for rural products, it is misleading to ignore the increasing importance of London as a major influence on the agrarian economy.

This is not so much a question of direct investment by London's wealthy merchants in agrarian development, though this occurred, as the stimulus of a rapidly growing capital to the remainder of the English economy. It is true that London could not have expanded as it did from a population of around 65,000 in 1500 to around 250,000 by the early seventeenth century, becoming the largest city in Europe with a population of 860,000 by the end of the eighteenth century (Wrigley, 1967, p. 45), without radical changes in the English agrarian structure. The eclipse of Paris by London may be taken in part as a measure of the respective strength of the agrarian bases of France and England over this period. Yet London – in its roles of port, mercantile centre, largest single market for commerce goods and capital city – had by the seventeenth century become an autonomous engine of expansion in its own right. This was linked both with centralization of communications and a shift from export-led to import-led commercial expansion, entailing a shift towards the provincial location of much production for export to a more centralized mercantile control of international trade (Fisher, 1971). The fact that London housed 7 per cent of England's total population in 1650, and around 10 per cent by the first half of the eighteenth century, has been linked by Wrigley (1967, pp. 45, 48) to 'great changes in the methods used on farms over a wider and wider area in the commercial organization of the food market and in the transport of food'.

In the case of Holland it is tempting to cite the importance of the urban network around Amsterdam founded on trade and finance, but also involved in industrial production and agrarian investment (de Vries, 1974) as indicators of a unilaterally urban-centred transition to a more modern economy. It is also possible to link this urban-centredness with the capacity of Holland to import a significant amount of its food requirements, paid for with the profits from trade. Against such perspectives, de Vries (1974) has argued that certain structural changes in the agrarian economy were of immense importance to the development of trade and commercial institutions. Here rural responsiveness (or lack of it) to market opportunity is treated as an autonomous variable rather than an automatic function of urban stimuli. Such responsiveness depends in part on the capacity of the peasant household to shift from largely subsistence farming with limited contact with product markets, to market-directed agricultural specialization.

De Vries argues that the buoyant market conditions of the sixteenth and seventeenth centuries saw a favourable response by Dutch rural producers with the transformation of 'unspecialised peasant households' into 'commercial, highly capitalised farm enterprises', linked with other local non-agricultural specialists. This depended to some degree on urban investment in land, and on expanding urban demand for food, but also on the historical legacy of a social structure in which the nobility was weak, owning little land, and hence where serfdom and seigneurial controls were also limited. This situation is not entirely successfully explained by reference to noble feuding and the intervention of the Habsburgs in the early sixteenth century, but it is clear that the position of the nobility in the northern Netherlands was 'uncommonly weak' by European standards.

Like Brenner, de Vries insists that market opportunity is insufficient as an explanation of agrarian development, since similar market conditions do not bring forth similar outcomes with different regions. French agriculture did not achieve spectacular advances, for example, during the sixteenth century when England and the northern Netherlands were beginning to make qualitative advances. The structure of rural property relations is also a common thread in the explanation of agrarian advance or stagnation. Where de Vries differs from Brenner is in positing a small-scale mode of agrarian transformation without large landowner sponsorship. In a more recent article Brenner (1982) identifies Dutch agrarian transformation as a special case, falling outside the English model, but makes no comment on the possible uniqueness of English agrarian transformation itself. He does, however, point to the subsequent eighteenth century failure to shift towards a consolidated industrial capitalism as indicative of the structural limits of the seventeenth century Dutch economy. One element of this is the greater dependence of the Dutch economy on external rather than internal demand compared with England. The implications of this are that while the Dutch faltered in the second half of the seventeenth century with the overall crisis in European society, the English economy was relatively more self-contained and more resilient.

In the effort to provide an explanation of why some succeed and others fail in transcending Malthusian limits, current debate has fused together the largely Marxist concern with changing agrarian property rights and an emphasis on the structure of markets in both rural and especially urban settings. In what amounts to a highly particularistic theory of transition, the pioneering English breakthrough is associated with a rural social structure conducive to innovation with markets able to expand beyond the servicing of craft-based luxury towards more mass-consumption items. While the relative importance of home and overseas markets or of rural and urban markets at various points of time has prompted a vast and somewhat technical debate (John, 1965, Eversley, 1967), what stands out in all such work is the necessity of thinking of town and countryside as economically interdependent.

The problem of rural proto-industrialization

It is well known that rurally based industries formed a major component of many of Europe's regional economies prior to the nineteenth century. What is less clear is the developmental significance of industries located in the countryside for the transition to capitalism. The fact of their existence in many regions of

France, the Low Countries, Germany and England has certainly been noted by urbanist interpretations of capitalist development. In general, however, they have until recently been subsumed under the rubric of the putting-out (or *Verlags*) system. Essentially urban-based merchant-manufacturers have been seen as the principle dynamic agency behind this system, whereby raw materials were supplied to small rural producers, to be collected from them in finished form as commodities for sale in the market. Although restrictive urban guild conservatism is usually seen as the underlying cause for the relocation of much industry from town to countryside, an alternative source of 'urban' enterprise is seen as responding to the constraints placed thereby on economic expansion.

This 'urbanist' assumption has come under challenge in recent years as economic historians such as Thirsk (1961) and Kallenbentz (1974) detailed a significant degree of rural and agrarian enterprise involved in the development of country industries. This theme has recently been explored in a more thorough-going way as a result of the pioneering work by Mendels (1972, 1975) on the rural industries and demographic structure of Flanders. This work which was organized around the notion of proto-industrialization stimulated a major theoretical reactivation of the developmental significance of rural industry by Kriedte, Medick and Schlumbohm in a study entitled *Industrialisation before Industrialisation* (Kriedte *et al.*, 1981).

There is a strong sense in which the study of rural industries represents an attempt to fill the conceptual and empirical vacuum that exists between those processes connected with the demise of feudalism and those identified with the emergence of modern capitalism. Given that the profound crisis of late feudal Europe and the decline of serfdom in many parts of the West in the fourteenth century did not lead automatically to the consolidation of a secure capitalist economy, it is difficult to accept that the solvents of feudalism are necessarily coterminous with the creation of capitalism. This leaves outstanding the problem of what happened to the European economy between the fourteenth and sixteenth centuries, the point at which England and Holland began to achieve significant breakthroughs in the transition to capitalism. Part of the answer is connected with the expansion of Europe's overseas trade contingent on new geographic discoveries opening up new markets and new sources of raw materials. The relative scale of this activity within the European economy was, however, comparatively limited well into the eighteenth century (O'Brien, 1982). It cannot, therefore, be taken as the decisive contextual change underlying transition to capitalism, even though it contributed to the expansion of mercantile wealth. In the case of England, the profits of the slave trade organized by urban mercantile elites did not make a very significant contribution to the financing of the Industrial Revolution, as Williams (1964) asserted. It has been estimated that only 4 per cent of industrial capital formation was raised in this way (Flinn, 1966, p. 46).

Another part of the answer involves those complex processes of social differentiation on the land in which the manorial economies of lord and serf gave way to peasant agriculture and, over the longer-term, to capitalist farming, whether by direct producers or by tenants. Many of the various Marxist and neo-Malthusian analyses of transition are geared to the strictly agrarian elements in this process. Recent work involving the notion of proto-industrialization has extended beyond this strict focus to look at the development of rural industry in the context of the resource base and social structure of the various regions in the early modern European countryside.

Proto-industrialization is defined by Kriedte *et al.* as 'the development of rural regions in which a larger part of the population lived entirely or to a considerable extent from industrial mass production for inter-regional and international markets' (1981, p. 6). The location and early initiatives behind rural industry – usually carried out in the domestic household – are, however, seen as largely rural. Rather than depending on urban agency, it appears that some peasant households moved initially into industrial pursuits such as textiles and metal working where rural under-employment, insufficient land, or poor soil made returns from agriculture, more especially arable farming inadequate. The combination of pastoral farming and rural industry, already noted by Thirsk (1961) for many centres of the important English cloth industry is further extended with examples from Flanders, the Netherlands and western parts of Germany. Rural industries expanded in many places in the late sixteenth century on the basis of the general population increase. In England this growth continued in spite of the subsequent decline in agricultural incomes during the seventeenth century slow-down or stagnation of population growth. Thirsk's analysis of the English situation remains important in connecting such rural activities to changes in rural property relations which encouraged farmer peasants or dispossessed small farmers to migrate to rural industrial centres. In this way a range of consumer goods were in production using wage labour payment systems prior to the advent of the increasingly urban factory age (Thirsk, 1978).

As with de Vries' (1974) analysis of Dutch agricultural specialization, the interpretation of proto-industrial development demands recognition of certain autonomous rural features of rural industrial development. There is no good reason to suppose that rural industry began solely as a result of urban agency, nor should one ignore the early importance of local village entrepreneurs or village capitalists (Braun, 1967). Medick (Kriedte *et al.*, 1981), has also noted the demographic and cultural autonomy and distinctiveness of the proto-industrial household. His argument is that the buoyant demand for proto-industrial products enabled family formation, fertility decisions and sexuality (including female sexuality) to be liberated, at least to a certain extent, from traditional constraints imposed by scarcity of land and peasant patriarchy. As a result, rural industrial households witnessed a lowering of the age of marriage and a larger family size than either agrarian peasant households or industrial proletarian families. By maximizing family size, proto-industrial households were able to maximize income from the extensive production methods of the proto-industrial system, while at the same time contributing to population increases which further fuelled economic development from the demand side. Finally, Medick links the independent rural artisanal households with the radical plebeian political movements that formed much of the subject matter of E. P. Thompson's *The Making of the English Working Class* (1963).

This argument provides strong support for the idea that 'rural air' can 'make free', and is a far cry from conventional theories of peasant conservatism. It is important, however, to note that proto-industrialization involved an increasing urban/rural interdependence. Proto-industrialization brought about pauperization (for example, in western France, southern Ireland, parts of Germany) where proto-industrial producers found themselves challenged by factory production from new regions. It is arguable that labour migration from proto-industrial to industrial regions represented another significant mobile source of wage labour within the transition to capitalism. In addition, at least some of those concerned already possessed metal-working and textile production skills. There are, however, very few studies of the cultural implications of the rural/urban migration process in terms of the possibility that migrants may have brought certain 'non-traditional' cultural patterns or experiences with them to the city. Rural–urban migration is still presented in terms of the entrance by a conservative peasantry, recently dispossessed of its land, into the dynamic of the poverty-stricken and anomic environment of the city.

While the relationship between rural and agrarian life and European capitalist development pushes up against some of the frontiers of existing historical research, there is sufficient data available to sustain a critique of unilateralist theories of urban innovation and transformation of the countryside. It is also apparent that the economic interdependence of city and country-side reflects their common (though often uneven) integration into wider patterns of production and exchange relations. What is far more problematic is the extent to which changes in production and exchange relations – subsuming town and countryside – can be analysed without recourse to the political changes that brought Europe from the feudal epoch to the era of modern nation-states.

CITIES, THE RISE OF THE NATION-STATE, AND THE TRANSITION TO CAPITALISM

In addition to the two problematic relationships between cities and feudalism, and cities and the rural economy, already discussed lies a third major difficulty with urbanist theories of transition. This involves the 'national' rather than 'urban' context of modern capitalist development. Is the modern nation-state simply the late medieval and early modern city, with its attendant *Bürgertum* writ large? Or is the relationship between cities and nation-state building more complex, perhaps involving domination by nation over urban autonomy? If so, would this negate or consolidate an urbanist theory of transition?

Neither Adam Smith's theory of the market economy, nor Marx's theory of capital accumulation explain why it is that modern capitalism has taken a national rather than urban form. It is as well, therefore, to be reminded of the problem perceived by Weber, as to the essential hiatus between the late medieval prominence of mercantile cities and the nineteenth century resurgence of a bourgeoisie within the expanding nation-state system of Europe. This hiatus arose from the fourteenth and fifteenth centuries onward as the existing autonomous jurisdictions of urban corporations were eroded in the increasing concentration of territorial power from which Europe's modern system of nation-states emerged. During this period the cities of Flanders ceded their autonomy to the dukes of Burgundy, a jurisdiction which itself became absorbed in the Habsburg domains, many of the Hanseatic cities of the Baltic coast became subject to the dominion of the kings of Poland or Denmark, and southern French cities like Marseilles were subjected to the rule of the kings of France. Elsewhere, major mercantile cities of the early modern period such as Lisbon and Seville, or Frankfurt and Hamburg, thrived on the basis of direct or indirect royal patronage. It was only in the interstices of the somewhat ramshackle Holy Roman Empire covering the Germanic lands that proceses of national centralization were sufficiently retarded to preserve some measure of autonomy for the imperial cities. While Weber exaggerated the evidence of urban jurisdictional decline, in his belief that 'the English city of the seventeenth and eighteenth centuries had ceased to be anything but a clique of guilds which could lay claim only to financial and social class significance' (Weber, 1961), similar processes of national centralization were at work in England too. The massive urban expansion of London at this time is not simply evidence of a buoyant social development, but also indicative of the rise of national capital cities as seats of national power, not simply of mercantile wealth. Trevor Roper (1967, p. 57) has characterized the expansive sixteenth century – a key moment in most theories of transition – as an epoch of 'eclipse' for Europe's cities, in the sense that 'the age of independent city culture is over'. The means of conquest had been the expansion of centralized royal or princely power, symbolized by the court. 'Essentially the age of the sixteenth century is an age not of cities, but of courts, of capital cities [such as Brussels, Paris, Rome, Madrid, Naples and Prague] made splendid less by trade than by government'. Trevor Roper does not, however, go on to associate the transition to a more modern socio-political structure in any direct manner with the Renaissance model of the state, characterized as it was by what he calls the 'carefree magnificence of kings and courtiers'. Unlike Sombart, he does not want to argue that luxury consumption had a major impact on the transition to capitalism. The evolution of a modern nation-state and the development of national economies is seen rather as a two-stage process. The first involves the successful centralization of the Renaissance state as a result of the erosion of autonomous urban jurisdictions and the subduing of the church as an alternative power centre. The second involves a revolt against the wasteful, fiscally profligate and parasitical structure of the court, whereby national centralized monarchies developed a more rational bureaucratic and fiscal structure. This process is associated with Protestantism – more especially Puritanism – with its doctrines of 'restraint' and 'the gospel of work'. These are seen as legitimizing the important struggles of the northern Netherlands (later Holland) against Spanish Habsburg domination and, even more archetypically, in the seventeenth century English Civil War between 'court' and 'country'. Where such struggles were successful the second stage of nation-state building depended on mercantilism, the protective support for the national economy in international relations in a manner consistent with internal social peace within the nation.

A final important component of Trevor Roper's argument is its controversial political interpretation of seventeenth century European 'crisis'. As we have already noted, late medieval and early modern European history is dominated by two major social crises; the first in the fourteenth century, the second in the seventeenth century. Whereas the first can be interpreted in terms of demographic crisis and conflict over feudal property

relations, symptomatic of the importance of agrarian transformation as a basis for further social development, the second,
on Trevor Roper's reading, is less concerned with demographic
or economic stagnation. First and foremost, the seventeenth
century may be read as a political crisis in the form of nation-state
development. Although not explicitly concerned with the transition to capitalism *per se*, Trevor Roper's argument implies a very
strong connection between the vanquishing of irrational
components in the Renaissance courtly state form and the
successful implementation of mercantilist policies conducive to
capitalist expansion.

The notion of modern nation-state building as an aspect of the
advance of rationalization, relevant both to the development of
bureaucracy and to the legal articulation and military protection
of capitalist property rights, is well known. What has proved
harder to determine is the relationship between economic interest or social class, on the one hand, and the form and substantive
policies of the early nation-state, on the other. One important
symptom of this problem is the difficulty faced by Marxists and
liberal-democratic theorists in determining the class character
and developmental significance of European absolutism. Such
questions are highly germane to the problem of cities and transition, because urbanist theorists usually seek to posit a positive
relationship between the rising bourgeoisie – meaning the class
of urban capitalists – and the various processes involved in nation-
state building. All too often, a mere rehearsal of the ideal-type
construct in which capitalism and the nation-state are seen as
intimately connected in the constitution of modern society, is
asserted as if it were serviceable as a historical analysis of the
complex pathways by which various manifestations of the nation-
state were conducive to or obstructive of capitalist development.
The main problem with this approach is the difficulty in locating
unambiguously urban economic interests and actors during the
early modern period, that can be demonstrated to have influenced the shape of nation-state construction.

The clearest case of such a connection is that of Holland,
formed as a result of the revolt of the highly urbanized northern
provinces of the Netherlands – the United Provinces – against
Habsburg domination. Dutch unity was obtained not by political

centralization but through a federal structure in which political power rested with local magistrates, usually members of the urban patriciate (Swart, 1975). Amsterdam, moreover, was in a dominant position, paying up to 50 per cent of provincial taxes and around 25 per cent federal taxes. This federal relatively low-cost nation-state suited the commercial interests of Amsterdam, but as Swart points out, it was achieved at the cost of effective centralization able to command resources sufficient to rival other expanding nation-states such as England and France. While closely involved in nation-state building and state promotion of commercial activity, therefore, this 'bourgeois' involvement did not lead on to the successful consolidation of an industrial capitalist economy. Instead, the increasingly status-conscious conservatism of the urban mercantile patriciate promoted its economic and political interests through a form of nation-state more closely resembling the late medieval city-states of Italy than the successful capitalist nation-states of eighteenth and nineteenth century Europe. As in Italy the seventeenth century Dutch patrician rulers became increasingly absorbed in rentier activity and public office. They no longer saw themselves as part of the bourgeoisie, but used the Dutch equivalent of this term, *burgerij*, pejoratively to refer to the middling sector of the population (Swart, 1975, p. 46). The irony is that Dutch fiscal and financial expertise in areas like long-term government borrowing was drawn upon in England's far more successful consolidation of a capitalist-oriented nation-state in the late seventeenth century 'Glorious Revolution'. Within purely Dutch terms, however, the strong urban-national connection did not in the long term generate a continuing transition towards industrial capitalism.

In England, the urban–national connection is clear, especially within key movements in nation-state consolidation in the seventeenth century. Prior to this England had secured both an effectively centralized monarchy and Parliament, whose consent to new statutes was required together with a local system of administration around justices of the peace. In all of this urban interests as such had played a limited role. Parliament, for example, was not organized on lines of estates, with burgers separate from nobles or clergy. Nor was the Tudor reform of the central apparatus of government dependent on urban pressure or urban models. During the critical seventeenth century, urban interests such as the City of London and many smaller urban-industrial areas did support Parliament against the Crown, and, in the case of the City, participated in constitutional monarchical settlement of 1688 (Hill, 1961, p. 275). This was to produce both fiscal rationalization or borrowing in the form of a national debt, and the establishment of the Bank of England. Yet the so-called City of London with its increasing dominance over private and public finance was as much a mobilizer of national capital, linking London with the provinces (Wrigley, 1967), as an autonomous urban interest. This is reflected in the increasing archaism of many specifically 'City' institutions as the national functions of the capital continued to expand.

In addition, the Parliament/Crown divide during the seventeenth century was far from coterminous with an urban/rural split. Many privileged urban corporations and monopolists supported the Crown, while large sections of agrarian society, including large landowners and small capitalist farmers, supported Parliament and the construction of a mercantilist state designed to protect and expand agrarian and commercial as well as industrial activity (Hill, 1961, pp. 102 ff).The heterogenous alliance that brought down Charles I, for example, comprised 'a commercialised gentry, a capitalist city (and) a commoner artisanate and yeomanry' (Anderson, 1974b, p. 142). Whether it is altogether helpful to call this a bourgeois revolution is debatable. E. P. Thompson has acknowledged that it may be a strain on one's semantic patience to imagine a class of bourgeois scattered across a countryside and dwelling on their estates. This derives, in his view, from an excessive dependence on the French Revolutionary model of bourgeois revolution against a feudal landowning aristocracy. If, however, instead of peering out through Parisian eyes, at the backward 'provinces . . . [we] think rather of the capitalist mode of production', he sees no difficulty in following Marx's view of landowners and farmers as a very powerful capitalist nexus', whose role in the English Revolution was central (Thompson, 1978, p. 40). While he is not averse to calling this group an 'agrarian bourgeoisie' he does so mindful of the eighteenth century urbanization of the status pursuits of the

English gentry, involving the expansion of fashionable watering places like Bath, Harrogate and Scarborough, coupled with the advent of the European tour. The urbanization of status pursuits is not, however, equivalent to the urbanization of the landed economic interest, though some steps towards the latter did emerge with the involvement of large landowners in the development of urban real estate. All in all, the English example does not provide a strong unambiguous case in support of the view that the nation-state was either founded as or was transformed by essentially urban interests or pressures.

In the case of the European absolutist states, any theory connecting the late medieval urban heritage with absolutist state construction must face a number of problems. One is the simple fact that absolutist nation-states emerged only where autonomous jurisdiction was overcome. The destruction of urban autonomy therefore seems to be a pre-requisite for national development, along with other corporate and/or seigneurial jurisdictions, whether lay or ecclesiastical. The capacity of proto-nation-states to achieve this depended in part on changes in military technology which made city walls indefensible, and in the scale and cost of military activity which was beyond even the wealthiest Italian city-states.

Poggi (1983) has sought to counter some of the force of this, by arguing that Europe's cities and town politics both 'provided a setting for experimentation with new political, administrative and legal arrangements that progressively penetrated the wider context of rule' (p. 55) and that the personnel of the absolutist state was recruited increasingly from a bourgeois rather than royal, princely background. In the case of seventeenth century France, he shows that the content of mercantilist policy often depended on previously elaborated urban regulations on business. There is much merit in this argument in that nation-states both drew on urban expertise and resources in fiscal affairs, and acted so as to universalize what had hitherto been the local and parochial structure of urban mercantilist protection. The latter point involves a paradox that the very process which saw the undermining of urban autonomy, such as it was, also transposed the urban focused notion of economic protection, onto a national basis. It may be inappropriate, therefore, to ask whether this transfer represents an urban legacy to modern state-building, or evidence of the developmental need to overcome urban obstructionism as if the two were mutually exclusive. What is important to stress is the lack of any automatic evolution from urban mercantilism to the development of mercantilist nation-states.

A striking feature of European transition, as Rokkan (1975, p. 576) points out, is the spatial location of the first wave of nation-states (England, France, Holland, Denmark, Sweden) for the most part outside the 'city-studded central belt of Europe, including Flanders, the Baltic and Western Germanic lands, and Northern Italy'. Centres formed, outside the domain of the strong independent cities that is 'on the fringes of economic Europe' (ibid., pp. 675–7). There was, therefore, no endogenous process of development in which late medieval urban estates gradually transferred themselves into national bourgeoisies. Flemish, German and Italian merchant capitalists did not evolve into national capitalist classes promoting the construction of nation-states. The fate of the Hanseatic league of independent cities is instructive here in that the economic bonds connecting traders as far afield as Novgorod in Russia, Bergen in Norway and in Bruges and London did not generate any political unity among the various urban mercantile communities. The league was not even a corporate entity with a seal and taxing rights. While able for a time to secure military protection by alliance with nation-states, the league was eventually overtaken by conquest and national redistribution of its spheres of commercial interests. Nation-states by contrast, including those founded on absolutism evolved not through extension of mercantile centres to national entities, but, in the main, by gradual accumulation of land (by inter-marriage and war) around an ethnic centre. In the later case of German nineteenth century unification, it is interesting that state-building proceeded not from mercantile and industrial west to agrarian east, but from the 'agricultural-bureaucratic core of Brandenburg–Prussia' westward. In this case a 'military stronghold on the periphery' invaded 'economically and culturally advanced [sic!] urbanised territories' (ibid., p. 577).

While there is clearly no single pattern of nation-state development connected in some necessary way with the transition to capitalism, it is as well to notice the weakness of accounts which assume that the nation-state is the proto-capitalist city writ large. What emerges instead is the importance of nation building as an autonomous feature of the process of capitalist development. One component of this autonomy is the notion of the state, more especially the absolutist state, as a source of rationalization. Elias (1982), following both Weber and Freud, has advanced some such theory linking state rationalization to both the development of the capitalist economy and the personality structure of individuals in modern societies.

Elias' analysis centres on what he takes to be a shift in political structure from a feudal polity of competing warrior bands, characterized by massive insecurity, to a court-based polity centred on the emergence of centralized royal authority. For Elias, it is the rationalizing components of life at court, centred on the development of a disciplined self-control evident in everything from table-manners to the conduct of sexuality and the pursuit of statecraft, which constitutes a decisive element in the making of Western society. This framework, which draws for much of its inspiration of Freud's conception of the repressive basis of Western civilization, treats the absolutist states of Europe which took over jurisdiction from urban corporations, not as feudal constraints to modernity, but as major contributors to social change. Rather than seeking out an autonomous *Bürgertum*, and organizing the history of the West around the city, Elias assimilates the civilizing of 'bourgeois' groups to the dominant courtly mode. The *Bürgertum* was present within the personnel of the centralized nation-state, but not as an autonomous self-conscious estate or even less a social class in the making. It was involved rather in public offices connected with government, tax-collection and the law and motivated in large measure by desires for increased status. In France, this produced the *noblesse de robe*, a status group of lawyers and officials of largely 'bourgeois' origins, distinct from the older quasi-feudal *noblesse de l'epée*. It was only in the Germanic lands where independent cities survived, and where distinctions between aristocratic nobility and urban life were sharp that a more discrete and self-conscious bourgeois estate consolidated itself. Being excluded from office and high status, however, this group had relatively

little influence over the development of society. This line of
argument is consistent with the more general observation that
nineteenth century Germany industrialization occurred in a relatively illiberal social and political context through an alliance
between the bureaucratic agrarian 'conservatives' and sections
of industrial capital more interested in state protection than full
liberal political rights.

The consolidation and rationalization of the state is not,
however, for Elias a matter of conscious intention. No new
legitimating ideology is required. Such processes emerge rather
as a result of the social consequences of centralized territorial
control and pacification of Europe which had by the early
modern period begun to demilitarize the older feudal groups,
and as the product of increasing national control of taxation as a
centralized monopoly. Such fiscal monopolization was a necessary precondition for the maintenance of the court and the
conduct of war. Although he provides no systematic explanation
of the underlying causes of national centralization, Elias men-
tions a number of contributory factors. These include the
supplanting of the castle-based, feudal lord on horse-back by
improved infantry techniques and artillery, and the shift from a
barter to a money economy, which enhanced the capacity of
those with territorial power to rationalize their fiscal affairs.

Elias' line of argument is important as a corrective to those
theories of Western history which link rationalization with the
rise of a bourgeoisie. One of its main weaknesses is the difficulty
in reconciling certain rationalizing tendencies in the development of courtly society in the early stages of nation-state
building, with the corruption and fiscally wasteful diversion of
resources from productive outlets involved in many absolutist
polities. Although attempts to check corruption sometimes
emerged from within, in measures such as Colbert's reform of
the administrative structure of seventeenth century France,
some account must also be taken of the Puritan-inspired
movements against the courtly establishment. In these instances
Trevor Roper's awareness of the limitations to courtly society as
an agency of rationalization produce a far more satisfactory
perspective on early modern European development than is
available in Elias' largely French-centred model.

Another inadequacy in Elias' discussion is the insufficient attention given to the extra-national resources often drawn on in the consolidation of particular nation-states. He tends to treat individual 'national' patterns of development very much in endogenous terms – the French socio-political structure pointing in one direction, the German in a somewhat different one. Among the issues reflected by this approach is the borrowing of political ideas and cultural models across frontiers. Europe was, after all, not simply a collection of discrete nation-states but also a distinct political and cultural region in its own right.

An important instance of this European context to processes of nation-state building, rationalization, and capitalist development has been suggested by Oestreich (1982) in his important studies in the consolidation of Brandenburg–Prussia. It is tempting to treat Prussian development as a particularly striking case of non-urban inspired development on the part of an indigenous centralized military bureaucracy. Prior to the French urban revolutionary impact on the Rhineland and the emergence of Rhenish industrial capitalism in the nineteenth century, Prussia had already secured a strong nation-state framework, extending its territory and feeding a growing population. Oestreich's argument, however, is that the Prussian bureaucracy, responsible for economic and educational, as well as military planning, drew as much on new currents of social, political and scientific thought in such Dutch universities as Leyden and Groningen as on indigenous Germanic traditions of military discipline. Bureaucratic processes of national centralization and rationalization within a state disparagingly referred to as a 'cabbage paradise' (Anderson,1974b, p. 265) was thereby influenced both by Calvinism and Dutch humanism involved with a revived neo-stoic political ethic. Oestreich demonstrates in a persuasive manner how the Stoic emphasis on a sense of duty, the importance of work, and the necessity of military preparedness made a profound impression on Frederick William and the Brandenburgers. It is also clear that the discipline of the Dutch army influenced the early builders of the Prussian state.

It might seem something of a paradox that the Dutch Republic with its loose federal structure should have influenced the military monarchy of Prussia. Oestreich is none the less convinced that the influence of the Netherlands in eighteenth century Prussia was supreme (Oestreich, 1982, p. 129). His comparison of the Dutch republic with Prussia – 'the Sparta of the North' – has the further merit of pointing out how the Dutch economic stagnation in the eighteenth century corresponded with a decline in Holland of the rational disciplined spirit of the seventeenth century which had so influenced the Prussians. In eighteenth century Prussia on the other hand, social discipline was already becoming built into the increasingly rational character of the state.

This example is important in bringing out the inadequacy of a national-centred approach to transition. But it is also instructive in demonstrating the crudeness of both princely-centred or urbanist theories of transition to capitalism. Prussian development was neither the exclusive product of a rational bureaucracy working from above nor an example of delayed development contingent on the belated arrival of an effective bourgeoisie on the historical scene in the late eighteenth and early nineteenth centuries. Oestreich's work demonstrates the inadequacy of explaining the 'rational' form which capitalist development took either as the exclusive product of princely control over cities or of the transposition of singularly urban ideals onto rulers.

CONCLUSION

The underlying thrust of historical analysis of European development is to undermine any strong sense of the late medieval and European city as an autonomous entity *sui generis*, and hence as a causal variable within the exploration in the transition to capitalism. The three historic issues surveyed in this chapter, namely the problem of late medieval urban autonomy from feudalism, the economic relationships between cities and landed society, and the problem of city in relation to nation-state each suggest the inapplicability of sharp distinctions between city and other social institutions. Late medieval cities were not manifestations of a wholly novel type of jurisdictional sovereignty distinct from 'feudalism' but were rather implicated in corporate seigneurialism. The heavy emphasis given to the emergence of a new *Bürgertum* or citizenry as a distinct social grouping is exaggerated and prone to anachronistic interpretation as a proto-bourgeoisie. The impression of the upper sections of the urban social structure is rather one of the fusion of identities as merchant and privileged patrician or 'trader' and 'gentleman'. Meanwhile, it makes little sense to sharply divide the urban from the rural economy, where this creates the impression of economic dualism between the progressive and the backward. Up until the end of the eighteenth century these two sectors are far too interdependent, and far more contingently connected with processes of innovation or conservatism, to justify any such procedures. If anything the urban sector was as yet far more dependent on rural advance or decline than vice versa. Considerable attention has also to be given to the agency of social groups denied a significant part in the urbanist view of history, such as the agrarian capitalist initiatives of large aristrocratic or gentlemen landowners and tenant farmers, or the rural industries generated by the response of peasants to under-employment and poor land. The important relationship between city and nation-state is equally one of interdependence rather than unilateral influence by one element over the other. The nation was not the city writ large, but neither was increasing national control over the city a sign of essentially extra-urban sources of transition. One of the implications of this is the importance of treating nation-state development as an autonomous and multiform element in transition rather than the necessary product of new class alignments posited by the urbanist theory of transition.

The combined weight of such findings suggest several critical consequences for urbanist theories of transition. In the first place, it is important to resist the temptation to over-compensate for the weaknesses in urbanist theory by articulating an essentially agrarian theory of transition. While there may be some value in counter-posing the nation that 'rural can make free' to the conventional urbanist bias of the old German proverb, to leave the critique of urbanism there would be to perpetuate the notions of urban/rural difference as both analytical distinction and established empirical fact. The second implication of this analysis is therefore to seek out organizing frameworks which are able to subsume ostensibly 'urban' and 'rural' phenomena within some more over-arching conceptual apparatus. One of the most promising alternative variables, within which what is generally taken to be 'urban' and 'rural' sectors may be subsumed, is the wider polycentric patterns of property relations as they effect the extension of a division of labour and the commodification of labour. This framework has been generated in the main through an internal history of European development, and as such is not necessarily sensitive to wider variables that differentiate Western from non-Western patterns of urban development. Above all perhaps, it is not sufficiently sensitive to the political distinctiveness of Western nation-state within which the occidental city became subsumed, in contradistinction to the imperial polities of the non-Western world.

All this does not mean the complete dissolution of any sense of 'urban' or 'rural'. These terms retain a limited importance both as demographic markers of the spatial distribution of populations, and as cultural symbols in terms of which many social actors organized their experiences. It is extremely important not to lose sight of the urbanist definition which so many have given to Western culture, since this offers a possible point of comparison and contrast with non-Western cultures in which such distinctions may be far less apparent. This 'weak' sense of urban and rural is, however, by no means equivalent to the stronger triumphant claim of urbanist ideology in which spatial distinctions correspond empirically with progressive and backward social and cultural spheres.

5

The Western city in comparative historical perspective

Urbanist theorists of transition to capitalism have never depended solely on an internal account of European history. Much of the cultural resonance and explanatory power of urbanist theory has been based on the proposition that European, or more precisely Western European, cities had a unique developmental significance compared with the cities of the non-European world. Such comparisons are evident, for example, in the contrasts drawn by eighteenth and nineteenth century observers between what they saw as Europe's dynamic, emancipatory urban legacy, and the despotic stagnant cities of the Orient, prior to European contact (Marx, 1965). It is not too difficult to perceive in such contrast a rather crude ideological legitimation of Western claims to cultural superiority. Further disquiet arises when the extremely favourable reactions of Western travellers such as Marco Polo, the Venetian merchant, towards the scale and dynamic character of certain non-Western cities are taken into account. (For Marco Polo's comments on China see Balazs, 1954.)

A more sophisticated statement of Western-oriented comparative urban historical sociology was provided by Max Weber (1968) in the course of his explanation of why modern capitalism and rationality developed in the West and not elsewhere. For Weber, as we have seen, the Western city with its purported characteristics of political and juridical autonomy on a rational legal basis, articulated by a discrete burgher class, contrasts with the internally fragmented, non-autonomous urban centres of the world beyond. Although Weber places some emphasis on the commercial and geopolitical dynamics of urban-based civilizations like Islam, he draws a qualitative distinction between Western and non-Western cities. Contrasts of this type have remained a prominent reference point in most subsequent literature on the role of cities in different civilizations such as Balazs (1964) and Elvin (1984) on China, and Hourani (1970) and Stern (1970) on the Islamic world.

The continuing vitality of Weber's agenda for comparative urban historical sociology is then an important reminder that critical assessment of urbanist theories of transition is not exhausted by closer inspection of European history alone. A number of major difficulties with such theories have already been located in Chapter 4, drawing on European data. Yet it still remains possible that a less triumphalist and historically modified view of the occidental city, set in the context of underlying patterns of social relations, may still yield significant insights into the question of why Europe somehow took a unique developmental turn at some point in the last millennium. This possibility relies on two connected propositions. The first is that the character of Western cities was significantly different from those elsewhere. The second is that such differences are of developmental significance. The latter proposition does not of course follow necessarily from the former. Beyond these two considerations lies a third. This involves the possibility that what may be taken *prima facie* as differences between cities *per se* can be better underestood in terms of some more fundamental generic pattern of social relations within which urban forms are subsumed.

From a methodological viewpoint, the comparative analysis of cities in different civilizations allows a check to be made on those accounts of European development which assume *post hoc* is equivalent to *propter hoc*. Weber's comparative research methodology was designed precisely to overcome this problem by submitting causal hypotheses derived from a particular context to cross-cultural validation procedures (1968, Chapter 1). Comparative analysis of this kind is, however, fraught with two kinds of difficulty. The first is the tendency to think of the city in any particular civilization as a unitary and unchanging essence. This danger is possibly greatest where Western scholars take non-Western cities to be manifestations of a traditional uniformity. Hourani (1970) has warned against this practice, in his emphasis on the multiform aspects of the Islamic city which varies significantly in time across the periods of the early Caliphate, the 'Turkish' dynasties, the Mamluks and the Ottomans and so on, as well as in space from Spain, North Africa and the Middle East to Central Asia and the Indian subcontinent. There is, however, a 'reverse' problem whereby scholars of the non-Western world may be tempted to treat the Western city in a stereotyped fashion as an essentially unique given in world history without sufficient attention either to the qualifications of urbanist analysts like Weber, or to more critical versions of the notion of occidental urban autonomy. Both reactions hamper comparative analysis.

A second related methodological difficulty is the imbalance in evidence on cities in Europe and elsewhere. Braudel (1982, p. 134) has noted this general 'historiographical' inequality as a barrier to the problem of the 'Gordian knot of world history' – namely the origin of the developmental superiority of Europe. Until the gap is closed – and very recent research has gone some way to achieving that – Braudel considers it difficult to define very closely either the extent and contours of European superiority or the chronology of divergence between Europe and the remainder of the globe. Braudel's caution, born of an awareness of the dynamic character of non-Western civilizations, contrasts in a very striking manner with Weber's well-known panegyric on the uniqueness of Western rationalism, written in 1920 as the introduction to a projected series on the sociology of religion. In spite of Weber's immense cross-cultural historical scholarship and linguistic virtuosity, there remains the suspicion that this massively influential text is far stronger in rhetorical power than in empirical backing.

THE WESTERN CITY IN COMPARATIVE HISTORICAL PERSPECTIVE

There can be little doubt that all civilizations in world history have developed significant central places in which key social functions are located and where populations have congregated, though not usually continuously across time. By the time we enter Europe's late medieval period from around 1000 AD, it is clear that urban centres are a feature of all the major world civilizations, in China, the Islamic world, and the Byzantine (eastern Roman) Empire, as well as western Christendom. If anything the scale of the larger Asian cities considerably exceeds those of late medieval and early modern Europe. In the medieval Muslim world, for example, the great capital cities of Baghdad and Cairo had populations estimated at between 200,000–300,000 (Lapidus, 1969, p. 61), while in twelfth and thirteenth century Sung China, the leading cities of Kaifeng and Hangchow achieved even higher population levels in excess of 500,000 (Elvin, 1978, p. 79, Balazs, 1964, p. 70). Such cities dwarfed the late medieval cities of Venice and Florence which reached 100,000 at best (Martines, 1983, p. 230). Moving forward in time, the great Japanese cities of the eighteenth century, Tokugawa, Shogunate, numbered in their midst Edo (later renamed Tokyo) whose population of around 1,000,000 probably made it the largest city in the world, in excess of London and Paris, neither of which achieved the one million level until the nineteenth century. Meanwhile, a second rank of Japanese cities such as Osako and Kyoto, with population levels of around 400,000, were comfortably in excess of all but a handful of European centres (Hall, 1970, p. 210).

In cultural terms, too, it is evident that the notion of 'city' as indicative of a discrete way of life was available outside western Europe. In the case of the Muslim world, for example, it is clear that many Islamic traditions focused on the city (or Madina) with its mosque, bath house and markets as the locale wherein a devout life could be achieved. Cahen (1970, p. 521) goes so far as to say that in the Muslim world . . . 'the whole of civilization' was 'found in the town', including administration, law, religion and culture. Against this strong view, certain cautionary comments have been advanced by Lapidus (1969). He warns of the danger of assuming that Islamic cities were sharply distinct from the countryside arguing that religious, communal and kinship ties cut across urban/rural distinctions. Islam was at least in part a cosmopolitian world. Identification with individual locality was, he believes, offset by this, and by the various modes of imperial control which dominated the Middle East from the tenth century onward. Yet having given due recognition to this, there remains an irreducibly significant distinction between the city as the centre of civilized sedentary life and the tribal world beyond. One manifestation of this is the distinction made by the fourteenth century Islamic scholar Ibn Khaldun (an observer of Cairo and North African cities) between the city as the centre of civilization, and the extra-urban tribal world conceived in terms of effective bonds of social solidarity and military prowess (Gellner, 1981). It is difficult to explain Khaldun's perception of an antithesis between civilization and social cohesion without reference to some sense of city as a social space differentiated from tribal nomadic areas.

In Chinese culture, urban/rural antitheses are less apparent. The predominant forms of imperial control tended to make little distinction between cities and their rural hinterlands in terms of the organization of administrative units (Elvin, 1978). At the same time a set of distinct terms for the city as a walled place or the city as a market emerged to depict specific types of spatial differentiation by social function (Ma, 1971). As in the case of the Islamic city it is important not to treat Chinese urban history as 'a monotonous repetition of unchanging themes'. Of particular importance with respect to the present argument is the evolution of Chinese cities during the Sung period (960–1279 AD) from political-administrative centres based on tight social controls, to a more diversified structure incorporating commercial towns and a greater mercantile element in the larger administrative centres (Ma, 1971). Such changes have been referred to as a 'medieval economic revolution' creating, amongst other things, a distinctively city culture with bookshops, bath houses, remittance banks, pleasure gardens and temples (Elvin, 1978). During the Sung period, Chinese urban life shifted from a culture based on aristocratic aloofness to one centred on commonness. This was manifest, according to Ma, in the loosening of social controls and the expansion of street entertainment, the wider use of printing and books, and increased social mobility engendered by the civil examination system for entry into the bureaucratic administration. Such changes were underestimated by Weber in his rather static conception of the Chinese city as embedded within continuing systems of imperial administration (Weber, 1951, p. 16).

If the existence of urbanized cultures in major civilizations outside western Europe is scarcely in doubt, it remains unclear exactly how similar or diverse were the cities of the world beyond Europe in comparison with the West. On the one hand, there is evidence that many cities across time and space developed significant mercantile, commercial and in some cases industrial activities in addition to political or religious functions. Long-distance trade for profit linked together Chinese, Indian and Middle Eastern regions generating distinct groups of merchants and merchant-financiers. Although internal political controls in China constrained Chinese domestic merchants more than was the case in the Islamic world, the evidence of long-distance commercial exchange and banking transfers across Asia is impressive. Looking at the situation reached by the sixteenth century, Braudel (1982, p. 134) sees no strong reason for differentiating the commercial development of Asian regions from that of Europe.

On the other hand, a powerful line of argument, articulated in Weber's comparative urban sociology, suggests that the political and cultural forms in which non-Western urban commercialism evolved ultimately made less developmental impact than certain unique features of the occidental city. At the heart of such contrasts is the claim that non-Western cities did not generate the same degree of urban autonomy as may be found in the West. They neither achieved significant measures of municipal self-government, nor produced city dwellers conscious of themselves as a distinct class or social group. The reasons for this, according to Weber, were twofold. In the first place, continuing tribal and kinship links fractured any sense of urban cultural identity and obstructed the development of class or estate formation on the model of the European *Bürgertum*. Secondly, the predominantly prebendal character of legitimate domination over non-Western cities depended on extra-urban imperial forms of political authority whose major tendency was to centralize authority above the urban community. In the Western setting by contrast authority was more decentralized, especially in the context of the decline of feudalism whose parcellized sovereignty had already left space for the emergence of autonomous cities.

The empirical basis of Weber's distinction between Western and non-Western cities has been criticized on several counts. In the first place, his emphasis on contrasts in patterns of kinship and culture seems rather dubious. The attempt to differentiate a non-Western pattern of urban culture fragmented by ascriptive clan or kinship ties from a relatively non-ascriptive occidental polity has come under fire from two directions. In the case of Western cities, scholars like Heers (1977) have pointed to the massive continuity of urban clan links with rural society for the late medieval period. In this respect it becomes open to question how far Western cities differed from their non-Western counterparts where similar clan and tribal ties undoubtedly persisted also (Aswad 1963, Baker, 1977). Although Heers (1977) points out that family clans within the occidental city coexisted with groups like guilds and confraternities, this more fluid pluralistic picture of the varied bases to urban life may not differ all that much from the non-Western picture. Here recent research has tended to dispute Weber's proposition that kin or tribal links typically overrode other connections with those of the same occupation or social status.

In Islamic towns, for example, Cahen (1970, p. 513) argues that tribal intermixture tended to reduce 'ancient tribal patterns to a sentimental link which became even further removed from social reality as the [urban] natives, whose importance was steadily increasing, did not adhere to it'. If Islamic cities were internally fragmented, as indeed was the case, this was less a product of continuing tribalism, but rather the product of a mixture of socio-economic, occupational, religious, and juridical-religious forms of stratification and residential segregation (Turner, 1974, p. 100). Meanwhile, in the Chinese case, Elvin (1984, p. 388) maintains that Weber's belief in the significance of the exogamous and endophratic 'sib' in producing a distinctive urban fragmentation finds no support in recent research.

It is also doubtful whether the strong claims made by Weber concerning the high degree of bourgeois self-consciousness of Western urban groups compared to non-Western mercantile and producer groups can be sustained. As we have seen in Chapter 4, Weber and his successors undoubtedly exaggerated the coherence and modernity of supposedly bourgeois social institutions in late medieval and early modern European history. At the same time, a weaker version of this comparison which dispenses with any notion of coherent bourgeois self-consciousness but refers rather to the relatively decentralized political and especially corporatist environment of the occidental setting is sustainable. Outside the West, there are few indications of the richness and integrity of corporate institutions such as communes or guilds, however patrician or aristocratic in ethos these might be in practice.

In the Islamic case, for example, there is little if any sense of the urban commune as a distinct corporate entity in its own right, enjoying particular rights or privileges, whether on a feudal or some other model. Islamic law in this respect developed no sense of the corporation as a mediating link between the individual (or individual family) and the political community. The Islamic world, while inheriting some of the imperial-prebendal forms of later Roman and Byzantine antiquity (Kennedy, 1985) is none the less to be contrasted with Western corporationist traditions. These appear to have emerged out of a fusion of Christian distinctions between church and state with Roman Law ideas of the juridical personality of associations.

Against the tenor of this argument stand the attempts by Massignon (1932) and Lewis (1937) to portray the merchant and craft guilds that emerged from the ninth century onwards as parallels to the autonomous corporate guilds of western Europe. These have been criticized as empirically implausible and far-fetched (Stern, 1970, Goiten, 1966). Although there are some parallels in the fusion of religious ideals symbolized by patron saints with occupational organizations in the two cases, there is also a sharp distinction to be made between the autonomous thrust of occidental guilds compared with the state initiative and patrimonial control which characterized the Islamic guilds. The Chinese case is similarly one in which any autonomous sense of an urban *Bürgertum* is lacking. As in the Islamic world, the overriding control of an imperial bureaucracy, reflected in market regulation and guild control, meant that urban juris-dictional or political authority was for most purposes absent.

In the case of the hang guilds of the Tong and Sung dynasties, for example, the merchants and craftsmen, while concerned to protect their common interests through occupational and trade monopolies were none the less controlled from above. They were used to collect taxes and requisition goods and services for the central government as well as to regulate and police economic activity (Ma, 1971, pp. 82–5). Hence although merchants became more economically powerful as a group they lacked any autonomous political preserve. This is reflected in what Elvin refers to as the Chinese traditions of 'urban political passivity'. It contrasts with late medieval and early modern European cities, which, however implicated in seigneurial modes of jurisdiction and however unsuccessful in combating the process of nation-state centralization, still managed to articulate political demands *vis-à-vis* other centres of power.

Research into the historical evolution of Russian and east European cities also tends to confirm a sense of the distinctiveness of Western urban patterns. In terms of the medieval period considerable debate has taken place over the question of whether Slav communities generated an endogenous urban sector distinct from Germanic or Byzantine influence. Much of this has been taken up with the question of how far mercantile settlement developed around princely Slav citadels. Russian historians such as Tikhomirov (1959) have tried to show that many key Russian cities founded round the tenth century, such as Novgorod, Pskov, and Smolentsk, bear Slav names, testifying in his view to Slav origins. Although empirically significant, this kind of linguistic inference is liable to the general methodological difficulty that non-indigenous founders may borrow names for towns from the surrounding environment. Tikhomirov has also tried to demonstrate the location of towns in the more fertile agricultural areas, rather than as mercantile accretions around centres of princely rule. In the western and eastern Slav lands, Hensel (1969) while emphasizing the plurality of such processes of town formation has none the less linked the majority to princely initiative. He does not believe them to be any the less genuine towns for this, however, but concludes that between 1000 and 1250 AD 'the towns of the western and eastern Slavs . . . developed, along the same lines as those of western Europe' (ibid., p. 59). This included genuine mercantile functions, a specialized division of labour and the achievement of town rights. The latter point is consistent with Tikhomirov's argument that the important city of Novgorod developed autonomous merchant guilds and urban political autonomy from endogenous sources.

The significance of such development is that Slav urbanism should not be read as a unitary historical process of 'Asiatic' or centralized princely control. In this sense Weber is probably inaccurate in assuming eighteenth and nineteenth century Russian cities to have changed little since the days of Diocletian (Weber, 1968). Istvan Rev (1984), while critical of excessively centralist interpretations of Russian and Eastern European history, has pointed to the increasing nationalization and centralization of Russian society. Whatever dislocations were created by the thirteenth century Mongol invasion, the longer term effect of the Orthodox Church was to support the rulers centralized control over society. Thus when Ivan III married the niece of the last emperor of Constantinople and took the title of Emperor, he had at his disposal the legitimacy he needed to establish absolute imperial power (ibid., p. 52). Thereafter, from the sixteenth century onward, Russian society at least became increasingly centralized, occasional uprisings of peasant-based movements for local autonomy being subordinate to the general thrust towards a subservient nobility, dependence of serfs on the state, and the abolition of the churches' free state. In the process urban centres were subsumed under one central pattern.

In eastern Europe, a development closer to the Western model was evident in the thirteenth and fourteenth centuries involving corporate urban privilege, and the emergence of guilds. The subsequent challenge to urban privileges in the East did not, however, produce effectively centralized nation-states on the various Western models but domination by a landed nobility whose immunity from central control allowed them considerable social dominance over the cities. In this way, the continuation of privileged urban centres, as secondary sources of local authority, depended on the balance of power between the landed nobility and attempts at monarchical centralization. Where the latter was effective, free towns such as Buda and Pest in Hungary, or Cracow and Gdansk in Poland, were able to retain a certain autonomy. The overall thrust of Rev's discussion is to show that eastern European urbanity fits neither into the Western nor into the various centralized Islamic, Chinese or

Russian models. At the very least this suggests the need to disaggregate the Russian urban experience from the various Eastern European patterns of development.

Although much comparative urban historical sociology remains at the level of rehearsal of sterotypical myth, there does seem some evidence in favour of comparative diversity between Western and non-Western cities. What remains far less clear is the analytical level on which such differences, muted though they may be, may be rendered intelligible. This is primarily because no secure or agreed basis exists for discriminating between different sub-types of cities according to their capacity as urban centres to stimulate or retard social development. The question then arises as to the most appropriate generic framework within which urban variations may be subsumed.

It is doubtful whether primarily economic criteria concerned with the allocation and distribution of goods and services are very helpful in making sense of the different types of 'urbanism' that comparative research into the various world civilizations has thrown up. This applies with particular force to distinctions like that between market economy and natural economy. For there is every reason to suppose that market-oriented commercial exchange for profit has been a feature of both Western and many non-Western cities. Notions of Asian economic stationariness are quite bizarre in so far as they ignore both the scale and innovatory character of Asian commercial practice.

The Marxist concept of the mode of production has proved somewhat more useful as a basis for identifying the various types of property relations within which 'cities' and 'countrysides' are located. The main thrust of much recent Marxist historical research, following Dobb (1963), has been to undermine any simplistic connection between cities and the lead sectors of capitalist development (Brenner, 1976, 1977, Merrington, 1978). The concept of mode of production has rather been deployed so as to emphasize the complex processes of stimulus and restriction obtaining between 'city' and 'countryside', 'urban' and 'rural', in the expansion of an increasingly urban-industrial society. At no stage in European development are urban/rural division coterminous with 'progressive' or 'backward' property relations as portrayed in some of Marx's comments on social evolution.

Marxist research has produced a number of important comparative insights into the divergent developmental consequences that tend to flow from different types of property relations. Such insights have, however, been more noticeable in analysing developmental divergences within various parts of Europe than in comparisons between Europe and the non-European worlds. The work of Dobb and more recent analysts of the European primary accumulation process has generally been directed at explaining why western Europe developed modern capitalism while eastern Europe did not, and why certain western regions did better than others (see especially Brenner, 1976). The extent to which the concept of mode of production is adequate as an organizing framework for more wide-ranging comparisons between Europe and non-European societies prior to the impact of Western imperialism at least, remains controversial and unresolved.

The most telling argument against this wider generic use of the mode of production concept is that its salience is restricted to societies where 'economic relations' concerning the allocation and distribution of resources are both differentiated from, and able to exert a dominant influence over, the remainder of society. In cases where patterns of legitimate domination do not rest on property relations but on some alternative authoritative basis, whether sanctioned by political, religious or cultural norms, the materialist connotations of the mode of production framework are less germane to the analysis of social change. While not denying the enduring significance of the conditions of material life and conflict over resources such as land in human history, this line or argument sees the criterion of property relations underlying the notion of mode of production as a particular type of legitimate domination, rather than a generic structure of universal significance (Konrad and Szelenyi, 1979).

Marxists have responded by denying a purely 'economic' interpretation of the notion of mode of production, and emphasizing the importance of extra-economic forms of property rights in the surplus extraction process in non-capitalist societies. This response, however, runs the risk of making the mode of production increasingly incoherent. The more autonomy is granted to 'super-structural phenomena' the more difficult it becomes to see exactly what it is that constitutes the enduring 'material' core underlying the particularity of different modes of production. The propensity for material determination to assert itself in the last instance is far too vague and spongy to serve as an adequate reply.

The fate of Marx's concept of the Asiatic mode of production is one symptom of the difficulties and dilemmas faced by those who wish to build a comparative historical urban sociology on a Marxist basis. The rather fragmentary and shifting definitional characteristics of Marx's own attempts to incorporate Asia into his theory of social evolution are well known. His picture of the Asian city as a 'princely camp' superimposed on material processes of production in the countryside is an extremely vivid and memorable one. Yet it is by no means clear that this picture of urban/rural relations represents anything other than a very rudimentary appreciation of the contrast between the geopolitical structure of certain Asian empires and the more privatized types of property rights characteristic of Western society during the transition from feudalism to capitalism. While problems of conceptual incoherence attend this bid to stretch the mode of production into a geopolitical phenomenon, Marx's discussion is perhaps most noteworthy for its rehearsal of conventional Western ethnocentric assumptions as to the thoroughly divergent character of ostensibly 'stationary' 'despotic' Asian societies from European norms.

Weber's comparative political sociology, elaborated and extended in recent work by Wallerstein (1974) and Turner (1981), offers a more widely applicable generic framework within which to analyse the developmental significance of different types of urbanism in world history. The essence of this approach lies in the distinction between the consequences of different types of traditional patrimonial authority. On the one hand, a decentralized mode – based to a large extent on the feudal institutions of fiefdom or land held in return for military service – while in itself unconducive to market exchange and tax-raising revenue in money, is none the less characterized by a parcellized sovereignty which leaves space for the development of private proto-capitalist initiatives. The autonomous urban jurisdictions which emerged as an unintended consequence of late feudal political structures represent the principal manifestation of this process. This political system is to be contrasted with a more centralized polity based on prebendal administration, that is, the appointment of non-inheritable lifetime office-holders by some central, usually imperial authority. This model deriving from Max Weber, which at its most extreme takes the form of sultanism, is held to inhibit private economic advantage and, more importantly, the differentiation of economic and political life except where it serves the overriding purpose of central authority.

Arguments such as this have been used to explain why it was that the urbanized Roman Empire did not accomplish a transition to capitalism. They have also been deployed to explain the limits placed on the development of Chinese and Russian cities towards some kind of capitalist system (Balazs, 1964, Levenson, 1967, Szelenyi, 1981). The point here is not that imperial cities are necessarily and literally 'princely camps' provisioned either by force or requisitioning to the exclusion of any kind of market or commercial development. It is rather that the development of market exchange, more especially the freedom to accumulate capital, deploy labour without hinderance of custom, or develop mass marketing, is constrained by political limitations on social action. In consequence, there has grown up a remarkable consensus of opinion in recent scholarship as to the salience of political authority as one of the most important, if not the primary, basis upon which Western and non-Western forms of 'urbanism' may be discriminated. This not only amounts to a rejection of the view that urbanism constitutes an independent causal variable in its own right, but also represents a challenge to those who take the material constitution of society as the foundation for the comparative analyses of urban/rural relationships and their connection with success or failure in the transition to capitalism. What is less clear is the relationship between structural political elements and cultural processes in the delineation of different types of 'urbanism'.

Weber's extensive though incomplete comparative analysis of world civilization combined a sense of political and cultural differences in his conception of the uniqueness of the occidental city. This had arisen, in his view, out of jurisdictional disputes within a late feudal decentralized patrimonial system, but also drew upon the legacy of Christianity. Part of this legacy, namely the acceptance of a differentiation of church and state – reflected in the distinction between Pope and Holy Roman Emperor – helped, however unwittingly, to secure a less centralized and more pluralistic polity where the model of the autonomous corporation was regarded as legitimate. Other parts of this legacy were more strictly cultural in that they involved orientations to social action. These included the conception of religious believers as a set of individuals rather than an undifferentiated community, and various forms of this worldly asceticism which reached their zenith during the Protestant Reformation.

While it is abundantly clear that Weber's Protestant Ethic thesis should not be interpreted as his sole contribution to the analysis of transition to modern capitalism, it is less easy to determine the relationship between political and cultural elements in his account of occidental history. Poggi (1983) has suggested that the 'political' emphasis on Western decentralization may be combined with the cultural emphasis of the Protestant Ethic thesis as interdependent features of the history of the Western *Bürgertum*. This perspective is, however, problematic in so far as it invests occidental history with a unitary bourgeois teleology that is at odds with the fragmented and discontinuous historical experiences that separate the late medieval and Renaissance urban expansion from the post-Reformation phase of capitalist development within the largely Protestant nation-states of western Europe. Weber's own position is less easy to determine from his comments on Europe alone, in view of the noticeable hiatus between his discussions of political authority (embracing urban autonomy) and its erosion by the nation-state, and the provenance of the Protestant Ethic essays which rest almost entirely on 'religious' rather than 'economic' or 'urban' evidence. Weber's comparative studies do, however, lend some credence to the view that overriding emphasis should be placed on the developmental significance of political structures rather than cultural orientations.

This much is evident in his attempt to come to terms with the apparent disjunction within the Islamic world between certain cultural orientations towards this worldly ascetic activity, and the centralized indifferentiated structure of political domination. 'Industrialism', for Weber, 'was not impeded by Islam as the religion of individuals – the Tartars in the Russian Caucasus are often very modern entrepreneurs – but by the religiously determined structure of the Islamic states, their officialdom and their jurisprudence' (Weber, 1968, Vol. 2, p. 1095). In this case, it is the structural consequences of religious authority which take precedence over cultural orientations apparently conducive to capitalist development.

The conduct of this argument at the level of structures of political domination rather than cultural orientations helps to explain why Poggi is misled in assuming that Weber's hidden agenda in the Protestant Ethic essays is the evolutionary history of the self-conscious occidental *Bürgertum*. While Weber quite obviously regarded late medieval urban autonomy as an important forerunner of late nineteenth century bourgeois society, he did so because he believed that certain Western cities at certain historical moments were coterminous with the development of modern economic rationality and above all modern rational-legal authority. At other times – especially those in which the nation-state undermined 'urban' autonomy – the urban milieu was not coterminous as such with these developments. This argument does not involve an 'ever onward and upward' process of bourgeois progression from estate to class because Weber did not need to posit 'urban' political or cultural structures as autonomous entities over the long term.

THE DEVELOPMENTAL SIGNIFICANCE OF 'URBAN' DIFFERENCES

Two propositions have emerged from the preceding argument. The first is that historical differences are evident between Western and non-Western cities. The second is that such ostensible 'urban' differences are rendered most intelligible at the level of structures of political domination. Whether such differences are capable of explaining the developmental divergence between Europe and the rest of the world remains less easy to determine.

The implausibility of general unilinear theories of social evolution makes it extremely improbable that a mono-causal explanation of this divergence could ever be adequate to the many complex patterns of change involved in the development of the major world civilizations. Having said this a remarkable degree of convergence is evident in recent scholarship as to the importance of variations in political structure in explaining why some societies moved historically towards capitalism and others have not (see, for example, Balazs, 1964, Baechler, 1975, Wallerstein, 1974, Braudel, 1982). Much of the case in favour of this interpretation has already been rehearsed. It consists in the observation that the pioneering transition to capitalism did not eventuate from the development of centralized imperial structures – whether in ancient Rome, Byzantium, the Islamic world, China or Russia. The various technological and/or cultural and philosophical innovations in these far from static civilizations were insufficient to stimulate change. Capitalism of a modern kind developed rather in the relatively decentralized West, where political structures were far from monolithic, allowing both internal differentiation between economy and polity within each state, as well as pluralism in intra-state relations within western Europe as a whole.

Further support for this argument is suggested by the Japanese development experience. This exceptional case of successful transition to capitalism outside Europe occurred in a society on the fringes of the centralized Chinese Empire. Tokugawa Japan (1601–1868) in particular was characterized by a relatively decentralized political system akin to European feudalism where local warrior-lords (*daimyo*) retained a large measure of local autonomy while at the same time maintaining allegiance to a central political focus in the Tokugawa *shogun* and court (Hall, 1970). It was in this context that urban centres of trade and industry emerged, the most notable of which was the autonomous port of Sakai, described by the Jesuits as the 'Venice of Japan'. In addition the various landowner-based administrators encouraged 'castle towns' as protected places of commerce in a manner not dissimilar to the town formation processes of feudal Europe (Hall, 1955). By the nineteenth century Japanese cities were large, economically diversified, and had high rates of literacy.

Although at least some features of modern Japanese transition have depended on external Western resources (for example, the borrowing of technology and capital to establish steel and automobile industries) it remains clear that certain endogenous features of Japanese society bear a very strong resemblance to patterns of late feudalism in the West. Braudel, following the work of Norman Jacobs (1958), argues that 'a kind of anarchy not unlike that of the European Middle Ages . . . developed feudal lords, towns, a peasantry, an artisan class, the merchant Japanese society bristled with liberties like the liberties of medieval Europe' (Braudel, 1982, p. 590). All this contrasts with the centralized imperial systems of China and other parts of Asia.

In the Japanese case, as in every other comparative case study, it is important to avoid the trap of assuming that all historic features of the society in question led inexorably towards the known development outcome – in this case successful transition to capitalism. While many dynamic features of Japanese society may be identified with a political structure which left space for the development of autonomous and relatively unconstrained economic activity, it is important to note that Japan's pre-twentieth century record in technological innovation and scientific advance was not strong (Anderson, 1974b, pp. 54–5). It is also important not to draw too sharp contrasts between the urban societies that eventuated from Tokugawa decentralization as compared with Chinese imperial centralization. The largest cities in Japan, as in China, were centres of consumption linked to centres of political power, where merchants rather than industrial entrepreneurs were of paramount significance. Braudel's evaluation of the developmental fate of various civilizations is not, however, based on a sense of wide divergences between those who generate capitalism and those who do not. He thinks rather in terms of 'small gaps' which may none the less be significant enough to allow advantages to accrue to one group and not to the other. It is not necessary, therefore, to posit massive endogenous differences between China and Japan to appreciate the significance of limited types of divergence stemming from differing political structures.

However impressive such political explanations of the transition to capitalism and the place of urbanism within it may seem, they remain subject to at least two major problems. The first

concerns the precise nature of what is meant by political decentralization. Both Braudel (1982) and Baechler (1975) refer to the
Western–Japanese political model as akin to a jurisdictional
'anarchy' leaving space for new forces. The danger with this is
that it underestimates the irreducible minimum of centripetal
coherence involved in these political systems that moved towards
capitalism. It needs to be reasserted here that capitalism in the
West or Japan arose not in the context of complete decentralized
breakdown but with political systems that had achieved unification without the same degree of centralization associated with
imperial systems. In short, this meant the framework of the
nation-state which eroded the jurisdictional autonomies of city
and feudal lord in the name of the monopolization of violence
and taxation rights over the population. While it is conceivable
that this 'national' phase may be interpreted (paradoxically) as a
development beyond earlier forms of decentralization, this line
of argument is vulnerable to the charge that this first stage does
not lead necessarily to the second.

An important instance of the failure of decentralized political
systems to produce strong nation-states – even where urban
centres were present – is to be found in much of eastern Europe.
The history of this region is very far from homogenous over time
and space. With notable exceptions such as the eighteenth
century Austo-Hungarian Empire, much of its history, especially
in the Slav lands, witnessed the ability of landowners to retain
sufficient localized power to prevent the formation of effective
national polities able to protect the social and political fabric
against external threats. This eastern European example is an
important corrective to the rather Panglossian view of landowners' contribution to the process of economic development
derived from the English example. Everything to do with landowners – whether in England or even more so in eastern Europe
– was not for the best in the best of all possible worlds.

A second instructive instance of the problematic side of political decentralization concerns the various free German towns.
These certainly retained a large measure of autonomy, but were
also highly parochial and relatively powerless developmentally
until the political unification of Germany under Prussian
dominance.

Such cases indicate that it is not political decentralization as such that is crucial for successful transition to capitalism, but the capacity to establish and protect a national political sovereignty. This involves an effective national polity able to limit the authority of powerful local interests. In the cases of early modern England, eighteenth and nineteenth century Prussia and Tokugawa Japan, the internal political structure produced a balance of power between central government authority and local land-owner authority sufficient to prevent unilateral domination of one by the other. In this way such nations were able to avoid both excessive imperial centralization and excessive decentralized fragmentation. National political sovereignty also requires protection from external threats. This does not necessarily demand a large centralized military apparatus as the case of England demonstrates. It does, however, require a minimum level of central coherence for purposes of military and fiscal mobilization, characteristics that proved lacking in the federal constitution of Holland. A geopolitical element in successful protection against external threat that should also be noted is that England, Prussia, Japan, and for that matter the USA all stood on the periphery of existing imperial or regional political systems during the formative phases of nation-state construction. Underlying all such considerations is the need to conceive of the political preconditions for capitalist development not in terms of anarchic decentralization, but in terms of some kind of equipoise between national coherence and internal political differentiation.

A second major problem with 'political' explanations of transition is their lack of attention to what is called the agrarian components of capitalist developments. These include the structure of landed property relations as they affect the prospect of commercial or peasant agriculture, and the balance between population growth and food supply. These issues can be subsumed in part under the heading of relative decentralization of political authority, in so far as such structures allow the potential for agrarian capitalist development relatively free from predatory forms of centralized surplus extraction. There is, however, no necessary relationship between political decentralization and agrarian capitalism, since such political arrangements

are equally conducive to local warlord surplus extraction or
peasant agriculture as capitalist farming. The serf-labour
agrarian estates of eastern Europe producing grain for European
markets are further testimony to the complex relationships that
exist between local landlord autonomy and capitalist development. For while fitting into a capitalist division of labour at a
European level, such regions did not in themselves secure an
effective national basis on which eastern Europe regions might
achieve transition to capitalism on a similar pattern to that of the
West.

The relationship between variations in landed society and
divergent patterns of social change is one of the most intractable
problems presented by the 'Gordian-knot' at the heart of comparative historical sociology. It is quite clear that inroads into
peasant labour immobility and low agricultural productivity are
required in order to sustain a successful transition to urban-
industrial capitalism. Since such changes cannot be explained as
the unilateral result of urban investment in agriculture, attention
is thrown back on variations in rural social structure and culture,
and in patterns of rural/urban interdependence. As we have seen
in Chapter 4 research of this kind has developed within the
Marxist analysis of European agrarian capitalism and in the more
recent debates on proto-industrialization. It has also been evident in the literature on Japan. T. C. Smith (1959), for example,
in his review of Japanese agrarian history has pointed to the
importance of changes in rural property relations in the Tokugawa period, leading to a commercialization of agriculture, and
increased agrarian productivity. Although this took place within
the context of small-scale farming often within the family
economy it did provide much of the surplus on which govern-
ment-induced Japanese development strategies depended for
tax-revenue in the later Meiji period. In addition, rural migration to the cities involved a labour force accustomed to wage
labour and in some cases rural industry rather than thoroughly
conservative peasant workers. Japan's transition to capitalism
evidently depended in large measure on agrarian origins, similar
to though not necessarily identical with those in Europe.

What is far less clear is what causal mechanisms and agencies
were involved in different cases of agrarian change, and whether

indeed it is possible to speak of a general pattern of agrarian capitalist development. In the present state of research this seems unlikely since agrarian innovation can be seen emanating from both traditional and more modern social classes – Prussian *Junkers* as much as English gentlemen farmers, small peasant proprietors as much as large estate proprietors. Since the desire to maximize returns from agricultural activity is consistent with a wide range of different cultural orientations, and since economies of scale vary considerably between the different branches of farming, it is doubtful whether the expectation of some relatively uniform theory of agrarian capitalist development is justified.

Political variables may help to explain, as we have seen, the mode in which the various agrarian sectors become integrated into international economic exchanges. They are also vitally important to the scale and distribution of fiscal burdens upon and between agrarian producers. But they do not adequately explain why some landowning classes or peasantries demonstrate a strong involvement in economic improvement while others do not. 'Market forces' may assist understanding of changing patterns of land use and factor distribution of income, but they do not in and of themselves explain why some groups within a given market context are more responsive to pressures of demand than others (Brenner, 1976, 1982). Structural systems of property rights and the political effectiveness of classes in maintaining them may help to explain such variations, but it is difficult to divorce questions of class relations from cultural norms and traditions regulating the scope and nature of transactions. Attempts to use 'cultural' variables to explain responsiveness of landed classes to economic opportunity tend, however, to founder on the grounds that groups with similar cultural orientations such as status-conscious landowners can be found equally among the ranks of agrarian improvers as rentiers. Even less is known about the influence of cultural variables on demographic behaviour, more especially fertility decisions, without which it is extremely difficult to piece together the influence of culture on population levels and the potential size and structure of markets. Explanation of the determants of agrarian change remains extremely elusive.

Such unresolved problems should not, however, obscure the

fact that the pejorative urbanist notion of landed classes as inherently backward and developmentally conservative has been discredited. In consequence the comparative historical sociology of agrarian social relations and comparative political studies stand together as the two most promising lines of inquiry in the search to find a means of cutting the Gordian knot. Neither requires an emphasis on 'urban' phenomena as such.

6
Cities and the problem of transition in long-term perspective

There is a sense in which theories linking city life with the development of capitalism represent one particular version of a more general thesis in which the city is connected with the advent and expansion of civilization itself. Etymologically both terms do, of course, have a common linguistic foundation in the set of Latin terms associated with citizenship and with the citizenry as a political community. The emergence of the concept of civilization in eighteenth century Europe (Febvre, 1973) involved a strongly ethnocentric view of social evolution. Defined in its most simple terms as a valued way of life, 'something great and beautiful; something which is nobler, more comfortable and better both morally and materially than anything outside it' (ibid., p. 220), the notion of civilization was intimately linked to the 'city' and to the idea of 'progress'. This set of terms were seen as depicting coterminous features of occidental history from Graeco-Roman to modern times. Within this ethnocentric framework, 'civilization' became a singular unitary phenomenon distinguishing the history of the West from various 'savage' or 'barbaric' societies elsewhere.

Although the notion of civilization has been critized as intrinsically ethnocentric and hence of dubious value to social science, twentieth-century scholarship has tended to retain the concept in modified form. In the light of comparative historical, anthropological and archaeological research, a more realistic ethnographic approach has arisen centred around the pluralistic idea of distinct civilizations. Each of these refers to a singular configuration of material, moral and political features shared by a major territorially distinct human group. The property of being 'civilized' which these varied groups share in common, remains, however, closely connected with cities. Thus it is not so much Western urban society as such, but the urban quality of various civilizations in Europe, Asia, Africa and the Americas which is taken to represent the dynamic core of social life in its various manifestations. Within the recent years arguments identifying the advent and expansion of world civilizations with urban-centred innovation or 'the urban revolution' have been enunciated in a very powerful manner by the archaeologist and pre-historian Gordon Childe (1950) and by the urban sociologist and historian Lewis Mumford (1961).

These general considerations have a considerable bearing on the specific problem of cities and the transition to capitalism in western Europe. If, for example, it could be shown that a general historical connection exists between cities and transition from one major social pattern to another up to and including the advent of capitalism, as is implied in recent work by Giddens (1981), then the argument presented above against the urbanist explanation of European capitalist development would need to be re-examined.

Giddens principal concern in the field of historical sociology has been to challenge the salience of 'economic', 'property right' and allocative power relations in pre-capitalist societies. Instead he sees such societies as fundamentally determined by political and to a lesser extent religious relations expressed through urban-centred forms of authoritative power. Giddens' claim, drawing on the work of Childe and Mumford, is that in most epochs prior to the consolidation of capitalism the city represents a major locus or 'crucible' for the generation of power, and as such is the principal agency of social conflict and innovation. It is therefore the city rather than the countryside which represents the principal theatre of social change in world history.

This restatement of an urbanist theory of history also draws in part on the work of Jane Jacobs (1970). She has emphasized the centrality of the pre-capitalist city to processes of social innovation, including the development of agriculture itself. While critical of Jacobs' economistic framework, Giddens none the less accepts her radical conclusion that landed agricultural society has never been the locus of power and hence of innovation and change. Jacobs' argument here is founded on the belief that the first cities emerged in hunter-gatherer societies prior to, rather than dependent upon, agricultural development. Agriculture is thereby seen from the outset as urban-induced, which in turn suggests an urban-centred interpretation of the first as well as the later stages in the advance of world civilizations.

The problem of the origins of agriculture, and the connections between city and countryside in the establishment of the major world civilizations continues to be a matter of protracted debate among pre-historians and archeologists. Two major interpretive traditions may be observed. The first is associated above all with the work of Gordon Childe (1950, 1960) whose thesis of an 'urban revolution' in the pre-history of world civilizations has commanded widespread respect. Childe argued that urbanism was the major common feature marking the consolidation of civilization in Mesopotamia, Egypt, the Indus valley and Meso-America. It was characterized by such features as scale and density of permanent settlement, division of labour, social differentiation, monumental buildings, writing and written records, and distinctive forms of social solidarity. This urban configuration emerged, according to Childe, out of the previous neolithic villages which concentrated on agriculture and to a lesser extent metal-working. As a result of pre-urban technological changes such as the wheel, ox-cart, pack-ass, and metallurgy (Childe, 1960, p. 71), such villages were eventually able to generate a sufficient surplus to support urban populations including non-food producers. An 'urban revolution' was thereby made possible. This allowed the wider diffusion of existing innovation and the creation of an economic and political environment conducive to further innovation. On this basis it seemed possible to argue that while the pre-conditions for urbanism were initially agrarian, once cities were established they provided the locus of innovation both in the oriental world and in the later transition to modern Western capitalism.

Childe's contribution to social change theory has been challenged methodologically on the grounds that it offers an ideal-type of a historical stage rather than an account of the processes during which the first cities emerged (Wheatley, 1970, p. 373). A further more specific challenge has been mounted to Childe's historical sequence from agrarian to urban on the basis of archaeological evidence. This seems to suggest the inadequacy of conventional views that settled agriculture preceded the first cities. Since 1945 a new theory of agricultural origins emerged, in which agriculture is seen as post-dating the establishment of permanent settlements (Perrot, 1968, Mellaart, 1975, Redman, 1978). This in turn produced an alternative theory of 'urban origins' which linked the first cities with late hunter-gatherer societies, rather than agriculture.

The argument is that where hunter-gatherers had become sedentary with a surrounding abundance of flora and fauna, a massive increase in institutional power and economic speciali- zation could take place around the settled area. It is from this alternative tradition that Jacobs and Giddens draw much of their account of the city as the essential source of innovation in both agriculture and elsewhere within pre-capitalist society. One serious implication of this theory for the transition to capi- talism would be that innovations attributed to the landed agrarian sector in the late medieval and early modern period should be regarded as essentially 'urban' in origin, stemming from the original urban construction of an agricultural countryside.

While there are many technical components of archaeological discourse which cannot be evaluated within the scope of the present study, more general grounds do none the less exist for doubting the veracity of the Jacobs–Giddens line of argument. In the first place, recent archaeological research has thrown doubt on the practice of sharply dividing hunter-gatherer and agricul- tural modes of subsistence (Legge, 1977, Moore, 1983/4). Rather than thinking of hunter-gatherers as the spontaneous appropria- tors of the fruits of the earth, and agriculturalists as seeking to control the natural environment in a purposive manner, new evidence suggests the two practices coexisted often in a complex symbiosis. Hunter-gatherers, for example, had already become involved in selective control over the natural environment in the late palaeolithic period through domestication of animals and systematic harvesting. Within this context agriculture was not a fundamentally new development but, as White (1959) points out, an extension and intensification of older practices of human control over the natural environment.

In the light of this it is illegitimate and unnecessary to consider cities as the exclusive product of a hunter-gatherer rather than agrarian society. What is crucial here is rather the recognition that either mode of subsistence, or in many cases a combination of each, may have been sufficient to generate a sufficient surplus to support permanent settlement.

Jacobs' emphasis on Catal Hüyük – an Anatolian settlement dated at around 8000 BC – as conclusive proof of a pre-agrarian city is also dubious both on these general grounds and as a result of more recent archaeological research on this specific area. Catal Hüyük cannot be regarded as the earliest city – with all this implies in terms of the theory of social evolution – as Giddens implies, let alone as evidence confirming his 'power container' theory of pre-capitalist urbanity. The first 'cities' of this type appear not with Catal Hüyük, or Jericho which appears contemporaneous with it, but with the settlements of Mesopotamia such as Ur, and Lagash some four or five millennia later. By this stage the combined hunter-gatherer/agriculturalist centres such as Jericho (Kenyon, 1957, Moore, 1983/4) had given way, in the Middle East at least, to permanent settlements supported by agriculture, but exhibiting a significant degree of religious and political centralization.

Up to this point, Childe's agrarian theory of urban revolution appears more plausible than the Jacob–Giddens argument, suggesting that the early dynamic in the history of Middle Eastern civilizations did not depend on some kind of precocious urban influence. It is, however, possible to locate further problems with Childe's argument, concerning the mechanisms that produced the 'urban revolution'.

The first of these problems concerns the explanation of why it was that 'urban centres', conceived in terms of the criteria Childe enumerates, arose. Wheatley (1970) in his comparative study of cities and civilization argues that a number of conventional explanations of urban origins have surprisingly little explanatory power. First, the variety of environmental terrains and climates in which civilizations emerged in upland Meso-America, non-tropical north China, and the mixed river valley and upland regions of

Mesopotamia throw doubt on the significance of any particular ecological component (Adams, 1966, Wheatley, 1970, pp. 268–70). Second, the significance of technological change as suggested by Childe (1950, 1960) has been eroded by research findings showing little correlation between technology and city formation. A third interpretation, stressing the formative influence of trade, has faltered on the difficulty of demonstrating that a desire for exchange is sufficient to produce those types of concentration of power seen as characteristic of cities. Given the predominance of administered trade in ancient history (Polanyi *et al.*, 1951) it is difficult to avoid the conclusion that state formation rather than city formation remains the more pressing focus for analytical inquiry.

Wheatley turns, as an alternative, to the consideration of the importance of religion not perhaps as a mono-causal theory but as a major component of his account of urban origins. Following in the tradition of Fustel de Coulanges, author of *The Ancient City*, he interprets the major common element in the earliest cities as religious/ceremonial. At first, village shrines and cult centres have no particular socio-spatial significance. Over time, however, some of them grow in significance as a specialized priesthood with an attendant band of handicrafts specialists emerged at one site. Such priesthoods functioned both as a major source of legitimate authority and of redistributive allocation of material resources, in so far as they collect taxes and construct new buildings within the ceremonial context. In this way the combination of urban functions stressed by Mumford and Childe emerged.

Wheatley's work is especially interesting in linking this developmental pattern to a non-technological theory of the agrarian origins of cities. This emphasizes the ecological and cultural instability of agrarian society faced with periodic food shortage generated by population increase, whether natural or by immigration. Such problems he believes produced a special emphasis on ceremonial centres dedicated to deities associated with fertility and plant or animal regeneration. For Wheatley, it is not difficult to envisage how those persons associated with the shrine to one of these gods of fertility, and therefore closest to the point of authority, should have come to mediate that authority and control the power derived from it. He writes:

Cultivator and craftsman alike . . . by submitting to the authority of the divine presence in the shrine placed themselves within the economic power of the ritual experts who managed the affairs of the deity . . . the farmer who once brought his offerings as a sign to the gods that they should begin their great work of fructification and who took part in the seasonal festivals that were for him nothing less than economic crises eventually found himself caught up in a redistributive system whose re-allocative demands were sanctioned by divine authority. (Wheatley, 1970, p. 305)

This interpretation of urban origins appears able to explain a far greater range of empirical dimensions to processes of city formation than Childe's technological framework is able to do. What remains unclear is whether the door is thereby reopened to the constitution of urbanity as an autonomous element in the advance of civilization in general and the Western transition to capitalism in particular. It might after all be argued that after the initial urban revolution was completed, subsequent stages of social innovation depended on essentially urban initiatives.

A major line of argument against any theory of long-term urban dominance in the development of Western civilization rests on the conceptual incoherence of the notion of 'urban revolution'. Within ancient history and archaeology a similar conceptual critique of the notion of 'urban' has occurred parallel to that in urban sociology, urban anthropology and urban history (see Chapter 2). This has proceeded in large measure through a critique of the belief that the city and civilization represent coherent coterminous entities. On the assumption that the major 'world' civilizations of Mesopotamia, Egypt, the Indus valley, Meso-America, China and the Yoruba regions of south-west Nigeria do indeed constitute discrete cultural wholes of a kind qualitatively distinct from surrounding kinds of social life, several attempts have been made to ascertain whether the criteria for urbanism proposed by Childe were empirically present in each 'civilization'. The premise behind this line of analysis is that if it can be shown that the various components of urbanism are not consistently present but only contingently related, then the idea of urbanism as a *sui generis* entity standing as the foundation of civilization is undermined.

Wheatley (1978) has once again provided an important synthesis challenging the coherence of urbanism as an autonomous component of and causal influence within the development of civilization. This argument is founded on data indicating the lack of certain ostensibly vital urban features in civilizations. The criteria of writing was for example lacking in parts of Meso-America and amongst the Yoruba. Wilson (1960), in his work on Egypt, raised the possibility of 'civilization without cities' arguing that ancient Egypt in the period of the New Kingdom developed a national political integrity within an agricultural land lacking strongly developed relatively permanent central places. In this sense he takes state formation, defined in terms of relatively stable patterns of political authority to be independent of any particular spatial form. A similar argument has been expressed in more general terms by Eric Wolff (1966) in his conception of 'cityless states'.

Such conceptual considerations reinforce a conclusion drawn from research on more recent historical epochs, namely that the 'city' is most usefully subsumed within structures of political authority and domination. Many further questions are left unresolved however. These include the reasons why none of the earliest 'urban' civilizations produced a successful endogenous dynamic towards capitalism. Another vital issue concerns the relationship between landed agrarian society and the urban sector over time. If social innovation beyond the neolithic period cannot be explained in terms of the progressive expansion of the urban revolution, it remains unclear exactly how long agrarian influences mediated through political structures continued to exert an impact, whether positive or negative, on the development of the various regions of the world.

In the case of European history, Lynn White (1962) has argued that the importance of agrarian sources of innovation, such as the plough or horse collar, persisted well into the Middle Ages. From the Neolithic Age until about two centuries ago agriculture was fundamental to most other human concerns (ibid., p. 39). He none the less takes urban sources of enterprise as fundamental to the eventual creation of a novel and characteristic way of life. The argument in Chapter 4 of this study differs with this view

– at least in chronological emphasis – by asserting the continuing importance of agrarian initiatives as well as agrarian–urban interdependence well into the eighteenth century. Equally important, however, is the specification of those forms of political authority, which distinguished Europe from civilizations in the world beyond and in which the various agrarian and urban components of the transition to capitalism were subsumed.

It is vital, therefore, to avoid a mono-causal explanation of capitalist development founded solely on some kind of second agrarian revolution – parallel to the neolithic revolution – and acting as a foundation for a second urban revolution in eighteenth and nineteenth century Europe. Rather the process of agrarian transformation should be placed alongside the distinct European polity of nation-states in a multi-causal framework of explanation. This political system not only represented the defeat of the parochial ascribed status aspirations of the burgher estate, but also helped to constitute rational relations between the state and economic actors in contrast to the various patrimonial imperial-bureaucratic systems within the major Asian civilizations. It is this pattern of political authority rather than any unique properties of the Western city as such which serves as the most developmentally significant differentiator between Western and non-Western civilizations.

CITIES AND THE PROBLEM OF TRANSITION IN LONG-TERM PERSPECTIVE

The analytical importance of injecting a long historical timeframe in the interpretation of the transition to capitalism is that it rules out that kind of teleological evolutionism symbolized in Childe's theory connecting the urban revolution with the rise of civilization in general and Western civilization in particular. Whereas Childe assumed that the modern Western city represented the most successful product of the urban revolution that announced the end of pre-history, it appears on the contrary that ostensibly urban phenomena vary so considerably in time and space as to rule out urbanity as a consistent, or at least periodically resurgent, causal entity. The point here is not of course that phenomena like the division of labour or writing are unconnected with social change, but rather that they should not be subsumed within some notion of historically progressive urbanism. In a very real sense therefore controversies over the problem of cities and social change are as much if not more arguments over the conceptualization of the significance of phenomena as disagreements over the empirical manifestations of social innovations and evolution.

The cultural and political importance of inserting a long time frame into the analysis of cities and the transition to capitalism is that it highlights the ideological character and functions of nineteenth and twentieth century Western urbanist thought. While the interpretation of transition remains limited to the analysis of Europe, or the comparative fate of major world civilizations in the modern period, it is difficult to challenge those world views which see cities and civilization as synonymous. While the metaphorical associations of the modern city either as a potential new Jerusalem or emergent new Babylon remain powerful, it is doubtful whether there exists any rational basis for associating the city as a socio-spatial form either with the means of social emancipation from capitalism, or with the incipient moral decline of the Western world. The major determinant of contemporary moral and political crises lie rather with structures of political authority at the level of superpower and nation-state, and with social movements seeking to bring then under moral regulation. The options facing civilization today are not symbolized by Babylon as against Jerusalem, but by nuclear Armageddon as against the universalistic values of peace and life itself.

References

Abrams, P. (1978), 'Towns and economic growth: some theories and problems', in P. Abrams and E. Wrigley (eds), *Towns in Societies* (Cambridge: CUP), pp. 9–34.

Adams, R. (1966), *The Evolution of Urban Society* (London: Weidenfeld).

Anderson, P. (1974a), *Passages from Antiquity to Feudalism* (London: New Left Books).

Anderson, P. (1974b), *Lineages of the Absolutist State* (London: New Left Books).

Aswad, B. C. (1963), 'Social and ecological aspects of the origins of the Islamic State', *Papers of the Michigan Academy of Science, Arts and Letters*, vol. 48, pp. 419–42.

Aymard, M. (1982), 'From feudalism to capitalism in Italy: the case that doesn't fit', *Review*, vol. 6, no. 2, pp. 131–208.

Baechler, J. (1975), *The Origins of Capitalism* (Oxford: Blackwell).

Baker, H. S. (1977), 'Extended kinship in the traditional city', in G. W. Skinner (ed.), *The City in Late Imperial China* (Stanford University Press), pp. 499–520.

Balazs, E. (1964), *Chinese Civilisation and Bureaucracy* (New Haven: Yale University Press).

Beaujeu-Garnier, J. and Chabod, G. (1967), *Urban Geography* (London: Longman).

Bendix, R. (1966), *Max Weber: An Intellectual Portrait* (London: Heinemann).

Bloch, M. (1961), *Feudal Society* (London: Routledge & Kegan Paul).

Braudel, F. (1973), *Capitalism and Material Life 1400–1800* (London: Weidenfeld & Nicholson).

Braudel, F. (1982), *The Wheels of Commerce: Civilisation and Capitalism*, vol. 2 (London: Collins).

Braun, R. (1967), 'The rise of a rural class of entrepreneurs', *Journal of World History*, vol. 10, pp. 551–66.

Brenner, R. (1976), 'Agrarian class structure and economic development in pre-industrial Europe', *Past and Present*, no. 70, pp. 30–75.

Brenner, R. (1977), 'The origins of capitalist development: a critique of neo-Smithian Marxism', *New Left Review*, no. 104, pp. 25–93.

Brenner, R. (1982), 'Agrarian class structure and economic development in pre-industrial Europe', *Past and Present*, no. 97, pp. 16–113.

Bücher, C. (1968), *Industrial Evolution* (New York: Kelley).

Burke, P. (1972), *Culture and Society in Renaissance Italy 1450–1540* (London: Batsford).

Burke, P. (1974), *Venice and Amsterdam* (London: Temple Smith).

Burckhardt, J. (1929), *The Civilisation of the Renaissance in Italy* (London: Harrap).

Cahen, C. (1970), 'Islamic society and civilisation: economy, society, institutions', in P. Holt *et al.*, *The Cambridge History of Islam*, vol. 2 (Cambridge: CUP), pp. 511–38.

Castells, M. (1977), *The Urban Question* (London: Arnold).

Chambers, J. D. (1953), 'Enclosure and the small landowner', *Economic History Review*, vol. 5, pp. 319–43.

Childe, V. G. (1950) 'The urban revolution', *Town Planning Review*, vol. 21, pp. 1–17.

Childe, V. G. (1960), *What Happened in History* (London: Parish).

Christaller, W. (1933), *Die Zentraler Orte in Suddeutschland*, (Jena: Fischer).

Cipolla, C. M. (1952), 'The decline of Italy', *Economic History Review*, vol. 5, no. 2, pp. 178–87.

Clark, P. (1976), 'Introduction: the early modern town in the west', in P. Clark (ed.), *The Early Modern Town* (London: Longman), pp. 1–42.

Croot, P. and Parker, D. (1978), 'Agrarian class structure and economic development', *Past and Present*, no. 78, pp. 37–47.

Daunton, M. (1978), 'Towns and economic growth in 18th century England', in P. Abrams and E. Wrigley (eds), *Towns in Societies* (Cambridge: CUP), pp. 245–78.

De Ste Croix, G. (1981), *The Class Struggle in the Ancient Greek World* (London: Duckworth).

De Vries, J. (1974), *The Dutch Rural Economy in the Golden Age, 1500–1750* (New Haven: Yale University Press).

Diefendorf, B. (1983), *Paris City Councillors in the 16th Century* (Princeton: Princeton University Press).

Diefendorf, J. M. (1980), *Businessmen and Politics in the Rhineland, 1789–1834* (Princeton: Princeton University Press).

Dobb, M. (1947, 1963), *Studies in the Development of Capitalism* (London: Routledge & Kegan Paul).

Dollinger, P. (1970), *The German Hansa* (London: Macmillan).

Durkheim, E. (1933), *The Division of Labour* (Toronto: Macmillan).

Elias, N. (1978), *The Civilising Process – Vol. 1. The History of Manners* (Oxford: Blackwell).

Elias, N. (1982), *The Civilising Process – Vol. 2. State Formation and Civilisation* (Oxford: Blackwell).

Elvin, M. (1978), 'Chinese cities since the Sung Dynasty', in P. Abrams and E. Wrigley (eds), *Towns in Societies* (Cambridge: CUP), pp. 79–90.

Elvin, M. (1984), 'Why China failed to create an endogenous industrial capitalism', *Theory and Society*, vol. 13, no. 3, pp. 379–91.

Engels, F. (1969), 'The housing question', in K. Marx and F. Engels, *Selected Works*, vol. 2 (Moscow: Progress Publishers).

Eversley, D. E. C. (1967), 'The home market and economic growth in England 1750–1780', in E. L. Jones and G. E. Mingay, *Land, Labour and Population in the Industrial Revolution* (London: Arnold), pp. 206–59.

Febvre, L. (1973), 'Civilisation: evolution of a word and group of ideas', in P. Burke (ed.), *A New Kind of History* (London: Routledge & Kegan Paul), pp. 219–57.

Finley, M. (1977), 'The ancient city: from Fustel de Coulanges to Max Weber and beyond', *Comparative Studies in Society and History*, vol. 19, pp. 305–27.

Fisher, F. T. (1971), 'London as an engine of growth', in J. Bromley and E. H. Kossman (eds), *Britain and the Netherlands*, IV, pp. 3–16.

Flinn, M. (1966), *The Origins of the Industrial Revolution* (London: Longman).

Foster, G. M. (1953), 'What is folk culture?' *American Anthropologist*, vol. 55, pp. 159–73.

Friedrichs, C. R. (1975), 'Capitalism, mobility and class formation in the early modern German city', *Past and Present*, no. 69, pp. 24–49.

Frisby, D. (1981), *Sociological Impressionism: A Reassessment of Georg Simmel's Social Theory* (London: Heinemann).

Gans, H. (1968), 'Urbanism and suburbanism as ways of life', in R. Pahl (ed.), *Readings in Urban Sociology* (Oxford: Pergamon Press), pp. 95–118.

Gellner, E. (1981), *Muslim Society* (Cambridge: CUP).

Giddens, A. (1981), *A Contemporary Critique of Historical Materialism* (London: Macmillan).

Goitein, S. (1966), *Studies in Islamic History and Institutions* (Leider: Brill).

Grassby, R. (1970), 'English merchant capitalism in the late 17th century: the composition of business fortunes', *Past and Present*, no. 46, pp. 87–107.

Hale, J. R. (1979), *Florence and the Medici* (London: Thames & Hudson).

Hall, J. W. (1955), 'The castle town and Japan's modern urbanisation', *Far Eastern Quarterly*, vol. 15, no. 1, pp. 37–56.

Hall, J. W. (1970), *Japan from Prehistory to Modern Times* (London: Weidenfeld).

Harris, C. D. and Ullman, E. L. (1945), 'The nature of cities', *Annals of the American Academy of Politics and Social Science*, vol. 242, pp. 7–17.

Hauser, P. M. (1965), 'Observations on the urban-folk and urban-rural distinctions as forms of Western ethnocentrism', in P. M. Hauser and L. F. Schnore (eds), *The Study of Urbanization* (New York: Wiley), pp. 503–17.

Heers, J. (1977), *Family Clans in the Middle Ages* (Amsterdam: New Holland).

Hegel, G. W. F. (1952), *The Philosophy of Right* (Oxford: Clarendon Press).

Hensel, W. (1969), 'The origins of western and eastern Slav towns', *World Archaeology*, vol. 1, no. 1, June 1969, pp. 51–60.

Herlihy, D. (1967), *Medieval and Renaissance Pistoia: The Social History of an Italian Town 1200–1430* (New Haven: Yale University Press).

154 *Cities, Capitalism and Civilization*

Hibbert, A. B. (1953), 'The origin of the medieval town patriciate', *Past and Present*, no. 3, pp. 15–27.

Hill, C. (1961), *The Century of Revolution, 1603–1714* (London: Nelson).

Hilton, R. (1969), *The Decline of Serfdom in Medieval England* (London: Macmillan).

Hilton, R. (1973), *Bond Men Made Free: Medieval Peasant Movements and the English Rising of 1381* (London: Temple Smith).

Hilton, R. (1978), *The Transition from Feudalism to Capitalism* (London: New Left Books).

Hilton, R. (1979), 'Towns in English feudal society', *Review*, vol. 3, no. 1, pp. 3–20.

Hilton, R. (1984), 'Feudalism in Europe: problems for historical materialists', *New Left Review*, no. 147, pp. 85–93.

Hobsbawm, E. J. (1965), 'The crisis of the seventeenth century', in T. Aston (ed.), *Crisis in Europe 1560–1660* (London: Routledge & Kegan Paul), pp. 5–58.

Hoffman, R. C. (1977), 'Wroclaw citizens as rural landholders', in H. Miskimin et al., (eds), *The Medieval City* (New Haven: Yale University Press), pp. 293–311.

Holton, R. J. (1981), 'Marxist theories of social change and the transition from feudalism to capitalism', *Theory and Society*, vol. 10, pp. 833–67.

Holton, R. J. (1985), *The Transition from Feudalism to Capitalism* (London: Macmillan).

Hoselitz, B. (1953), 'The role of cities in the economic growth of underdeveloped countries', *Journal of Political Economy*, vol. 6, pp. 195–208.

Hourani, A. H. (1970), 'The Islamic city in the light of recent research', in A. Hourani and S. Stern (eds), *The Islamic City* (Oxford: Bruno Cassirer), pp. 9–24.

Jacobs, J. (1970), *The Economy of Cities* (London: Cape).

Jacobs, N. (1958), *The Origin of Modern Capitalism and East Asia* (Hong Kong: Hong Kong University Press).

John, A. H. (1965), 'Agricultural productivity and economic growth in England 1700–1760', *Journal of Economic History*, vol. 25, pp. 19–34.

Jones, A. H. M. (1966), *The Greek City from Alexander to Justinian* (Oxford: Clarendon Press).

Jones, E. (1966), *Towns and Cities* (Oxford: OUP).

Kallenbentz, H. (1974), 'Rural industries from the end of the middle ages to the 18th century', in P. Earle (ed.), *Essays in European Economic History 1500–1800* (Oxford: Clarendon Press), pp. 45–88.

Kennedy, H. (1985), 'From Polis to Madina: urban change in late antique and early Islamic Syria', *Past and Present*, no. 106, pp. 3–27.

Kenyon, K. (1957), *Digging Up Jericho* (New York: Praeger).

Konrad, G. and Szelenyi, I. (1979), *The Intellectuals on the Road to Class Power* (Brighton: Harvester).

Koselleck, R. (1982), 'Begriffsgeschichte and social history', *Economy and Society*, vol. 11, no. 4, pp. 409–27.

Kriedte, P., Medick, H. and Schlumbohm, J. (1981), *Industrialisation before Industrialisation* (Cambridge: CUP).

Langton, J. (1982), 'The behavioural theory of evolution and the Weber thesis', *Sociology*, vol. 16, no. 4, pp. 341–58.

Lapidus, I. (1969), 'Muslim cities and Islamic societies', in I. Lapidus (ed.), *Middle Eastern Cities* (Berkeley: University of California Press), pp. 47–79.

Lefebvre, H. (1972), *La Pensée Marxiste et la ville* (Paris: Casterman).

Lefebvre, H. (1976), *The Survival of Capitalism* (London: Allison and Busby).

Legge, A. J. (1977), 'The origins of agriculture in the Near East', in J. V. Megaw (ed.), *Hunters, Gatherers and First Farmers Beyond Europe* (Leicester: Leicester University Press), pp. 51–68.

Le Goff, J. (1972), 'The town as an agent of civilisation c1200–c1500', in C. Cipolla (ed.), *Fontana Economic History of Europe: Vol. 1, The Middle Ages* (London: Collins), pp. 71–106.

Lerner, D. (1958), *The Passing of Traditional Society* (New York: Free Press).

Le Roy Ladurie, E. (1969), *Les paysans de Languedoc* (Paris: Flammarion).

Le Roy Ladurie, E. (1974), 'L'histoire immobile', *Annales ESC*, vol. 29, pp. 673–92.

Le Roy Ladurie, E. (1978a). *Montaillou* (London: Scolar Press).

Le Roy Ladurie, E. (1978b), 'A reply to Professor Brenner', *Past and Present*, no. 79, pp. 55–9.

Leveau, P. (1983), 'La ville antique et l'organisation de l'espace rural: villa, ville, village', *Annales ESC*, vol. 38, no. 4 (Juillet/Aout), pp. 920–42.

Levenson, J. R. (ed.) (1967), *European Expansion and the Counter-Expansion of Asia 1300–1600* (Englewood Cliffs: Prentice Hall).

Lewis, B. (1937), 'The Islamic guilds', *Economic History Review*, vol. 8, no. 1, pp. 20–37.

Lopez, R. (1963), 'The crossroads within the wall', in O. Handlin and H. Burchard (eds), *The Historian and the City* (Cambridge, Mass.: Harvard University Press), pp. 27–43.

Lyon, B. (1974), *Henri Pirenne: A Biographical and Intellectual Study* (Ghent: Story-Scientia).

Ma, L. J. C. (1971), *Commercial Development and Urban Change in Sung China (960–1279)* (Ann Arbor: University of Michigan).

Macfarlane, A. (1978), *The Origins of English Individualism* (Oxford: Blackwell).

Martines, L. (1983), *Power and Imagination: City-States in Renaissance Italy* (London: Penguin).

Marx, K. (1959), *Capital*, vol. 3 (London: Lawrence & Wishart).

Marx, K. (1965a), *Capital*, vol. 1 (Moscow: Progress Publishers).

156   *Cities, Capitalism and Civilization*

Marx, K. (1965b), *Pre-capitalist Economic Formations* (New York: International Publishers).
Marx, K. and Engels, F. (1962), 'The Communist Manifesto', in *Selected Works*, vol. 1 (Moscow: Progress Publishers).
Marx, K. and Engels, F. (1976), *The German Ideology* (Moscow: Progress Publishers).
Massingnon, L. (1932), 'Guilds (Islamic)', in *Encyclopaedia of the Social Sciences* (London: Macmillan), pp. 214–16.
Mellaart, L. (1975), *The Neolithic of the Near East* (London: Thames & Hudson).
Mendels, F. (1972), 'Proto-industrialisation. The first phase of the industrialisation process', *Journal of Economic History*, vol. 32, pp. 241–61.
Mendels, F. (1975), 'Agriculture and peasant industry in 18th century Flanders', in W. N. Parker and E. L. Jones (eds), *European Peasants and Their Markets* (Princeton: Princeton University Press).
Merrington, J. (1975), 'Town and country in the transition to capitalism', *New Left Review*, no. 93 (September–October), pp. 71–92.
Mickwitz, G. (1936), *Die Kartellfunktionen der Zünfte und ihre Bedeutung bei der Enstehung des Zunftwesens* (Helsinki: Finska Vetenshaps-societen).
Moore, A. M. T. (1983/4), 'Agricultural origins in the Near East', *World Archaeology*, vol. 14, pp. 224–36.
Moore, B. (1966), *Social Origins of Dictatorship and Democracy* (Boston: Beacon Press).
Mumford, L. (1961), *The City in History* (New York: Harcourt Brace).
Mussett, L. (1975), *The Germanic Invasions* (London: Elek).
Nicholas, D. M. (1968), 'Town and countryside: social and economic tensions in 14th century Flanders', *Comparative Studies in Society and History*, vol. 10, pp. 458–85.
Nicholas, D. M. (1971), *Town and Countryside: Social, Economic and Political Tensions in 14th Century Flanders* (Bruges: De Tempel).
Nicholas, D. (1976), 'Economic reorientation and social change in fourteenth-century Flanders', *Past and Present*, no. 70, pp. 3–29.
O'Brien, P. (1982), 'European overseas development: the contribution of the periphery', *Economic History Review*, vol. 35, no. 1, pp. 1–18.
Oestreich, G. (1982), *Neostoicism and the Early Modern State* (Cambridge: CUP).
Pahl, R. (1968), 'The rural-urban continuum', in R. Pahl (ed.), *Readings in Urban Sociology* (Oxford: Pergamon Press), pp. 263–305.
Parsons, T. (1971), *The System of Modern Societies* (Englewood Cliffs: Prentice Hall).
Perrot, J. (1968), 'La préhistoire palestinienne' in Letovzey, L. and Ane, J. *Supplement au Dictionnaire de la Bible 8*, cols 286–46.
Pickvance, C. (1976), 'Introduction: historical materialist approaches to urban sociology', in C. Pickvance (ed.), *Urban Sociology* (London: Tavistock).

Pirenne, J. (1913–14), 'The stages in the social history of capitalism', *American Historical Review*, vol. 19, pp. 494–515.
Pirenne, H. (1925), *Medieval Cities* (Princeton: Princeton University Press).
Pirenne, H. (1963), *Early Democracies in the Low Countries* (New York: Harper & Row).
Plant, R. (1973), *Hegel* (London: Allen & Unwin).
Poggi, G. (1978), *The Development of the Modern State* (London: Hutchinson).
Poggi, G. (1983), *Calvinism and the Capitalist Spirit* (London: Macmillan).
Polanyi, K., Arensberg, C. and Pearson, H. (1957), *Trade and Market in the Early Empires* (Glencoe: Free Press).
Polanyi, K. (1977), *The Livelihood of Man* (New York: Academic Press).
Postan, M. M. (1950), 'Some economic evidence of declining population in the late Middle Ages, *Economic History Review*, no. 2, pp. 221–46.
Postan, M. M. (1972), *The Medieval Economy and Society* (London: Weidenfeld & Nicolson).
Postan, M. M. (1973), *Essays on Medieval Agricultural and General Problems of the Medieval Economy* (Cambridge: CUP).
Redman, C. L. (1978), *The Rise of Civilization* (San Francisco: Freeman).
Reissman, L. (1964), *The Urban Process* (New York: Free Press).
Rev, I. (1984), 'Local autonomy or centralism – when was the original sin committed?', *International Journal of Urban and Regional Research*, vol. 8, no. 1, pp. 38–63.
Riedel, M. (1975), 'Bürger, Staatsbürger, Bürgertum', in O. Brunner *et al.*, *Geschichtliche Grundbegriffe*, Bd. I (Stuttgart: Klett Cotta), pp. 672–723.
Rokkan, S. (1975), 'Dimensions of state formation and nation-building', in C. Tilly (ed.), *The Formation of National States in Western Europe* (Princeton: Princeton University Press), pp. 562–600.
Roth, G. (1976), 'History and sociology in the work of Max Weber', *British Journal of Sociology*, vol. 27, no. 3, pp. 306–18.
Rudé, G. (1964), *The Crowd in History, 1730–1848* (New York: Wiley).
Russell, J. C. (1972), 'Population in Europe 500–1500', in C. Cipolla (ed.), *The Fontana Economic History of Europe* (London: Collins), pp. 25–70.
Sahlins, S. D. and Service, E. (1960), *Evolution and Culture* (Ann Arbor: University of Michigan Press), pp. 12–24.
St. Augustine (1984), *The City of God* (London: Penguin).
Saunders, P. (1981), *Social Theory and the Urban Question* (London: Hutchinson).
Schorske, C. E. (1963), 'The idea of the city in European thought', in O. Handlin and J. Burchard (eds), *The Historian and the City* (Cambridge, Mass.: MIT Press), pp. 95–114.
Sièyes, A. (1963), *What Is the Third Estate?* (London: Pall Mall Press).

Sjoberg, G. (1960), *The Pre-industrial City, Past and Present* (Glencoe: Free Press).

Smith, A. (1976), *Wealth of Nations* (Oxford: Clarendon Press).

Smith, T. C. (1959), *The Agrarian Origins of Modern Japan* (Stanford: Stanford University Press).

Stern, S. M. (1970), 'The constitution of the Islamic city', in A. Hourani and S. Stern (eds), *The Islamic City* (Oxford: Cassirer), pp. 25–50.

Stewart, C. T. (1958), 'The urban-rural dichotomy: concepts and uses', *American Journal of Sociology*, vol. 64, pp. 152–8.

Swart, K. W. (1975), 'Holland's bourgeoisie and the retarded industrialisation of the Netherlands', in F. Krantz and P. M. Hohenberg (eds), *Failed Transitions to Modern Industrial Society: Renaissance Italy and Seventeenth Century Holland* (Montreal: ICES), pp. 44–8.

Szelenyi, I. (1981), 'Urban development and regional management in Eastern Europe', *Theory and Society*, vol. 10, pp. 169–206.

Tenbruck, F. H. (1975), 'Das Werk Max Webers', *Kölner Zeitschrift für Soziologie und Sozialpsychologie*, 27, pp. 663–702.

Thirsk, J. (1961), 'Industries in the countryside', in F. J. Fisher (ed.), *Essays in the Economic and Social History of Tudor and Stuart England* (Cambridge: CUP), pp. 70–88.

Thirsk, J. (1978), *Economic Policy and Projects: The Development of a Consumer Society in Early Modern England* (Oxford: OUP).

Thompson, E. P. (1963), *The Making of the English Working Class* (London: Gollancz).

Thompson, E. P. (1978), 'The peculiarities of the English', in E. P. Thompson, *The Poverty of Theory* (London: Merlin Press).

Thrupp, S. (1948), *The Merchant Class of Medieval London* (Ann Arbor: University of Michigan).

Thrupp, S. (1963), 'The Gilds', in M. H. Postan and E. E. Rich (eds), *Cambridge Economic History of Europe*, vol. 3, pp. 230–80.

Tikhomirov, M. (1959), *The Towns of Ancient Rus* (Moscow: Foreign Languages Publishing House).

Toynbee, A. (1884), *Lectures on the Industrial Revolution of the 18th Century in England* (London: Rivingtons).

Trevor Roper, H. (1967), 'The general crisis of the seventeenth century', in Trevor Roper, *Religion, the Reformation and Social Change* (London: Macmillan), pp. 46–89.

Turner, B. (1974), *Weber and Islam* (London: Routledge & Kegan Paul).

Turner, B. (1981), *For Weber* (London: Routledge & Kegan Paul).

Unwin, G. (1927), 'The medieval city', in G. Unwin, *Studies in Economic History* (London: Macmillan), pp. 49–91.

Von Grunebaum, G. E. (1970), 'The sources of Islamic civilisation', in P. M. Holt *et al.*, *Cambridge History of Islam: Vol. 2* (Cambridge: CUP), pp. 469–510.

Von Stromer, W. (1981), 'Commercial policy and economic conjuncture in Nuremburg at the close of the Middle Ages: a model of economic policy', *Journal of European Economic History*, vol. 10, no. 1, pp. 119–29.

Waley, D. (1969), *The Italian City-Republics* (London: Weidenfeld & Nicholson).

Walker, M. (1971), *German Home Towns: Community, State and General Estate 1648–1871* (Ithaca: Cornell University Press).

Wallerstein, I. (1974), *The Modern World System, Vol. 1* (New York: Academic Press).

Wallerstein, L. (1984), 'Cities in socialist theory', *International Journal of Urban and Regional Research*, vol. 8, no. 1, pp. 64–72.

Weber, M. (1924), 'Zur Geshichte der Handelsgesellschaften im Mittelalter', in *Gesammelte Aufsätze zur Sozial-und Wirtschaftsgeshichte'* (Tübingen: Mohr), pp. 312–443.

Weber, M. (1951), *The Religion of China: Confucianism and Taoism* (Glencoe: Free Press).

Weber, M. (1961), *General Economic History* (New York: Collier).

Weber, M. (1968), *Economy and Society, 2 vols.* (Berkeley: University of California Press).

Weber, M. (1978), *Selections in Translation*, edited by W. G. Runciman (Cambridge: CUP).

Wheatley, P. (1970), *The Pivot of Four Quarters* (Edinburgh: University of Edinburgh Press).

Wheatley, P. (1972), 'The concept of urbanism', in P. J. Ucko, R. Tringham and G. Dimbleby, *Man, Settlement and Urbanism* (London: Duckworth), pp. 601–37.

White, L. (1959), *The Evolution of Culture* (New York: McGraw-Hill).

White, Lynn (1962), *Medieval Technology and Social Change* (Oxford: Clarendon Press).

Williams, W. E. (1964), *Capitalism and Slavery* (London: Deutsch).

Williams. G. (1963), *Medieval London, From Commune to Capital* (London: Athlone Press).

Williams, R. (1975), *The Country and the City* (London: Paladin).

Wilson, E. (1960), in C. Kraeling and R. Adams (eds), *City Invincible* (Chicago: University of Chicago Press).

Wirth, L. (1938), 'Urbanism as a way of life', *American Journal of Sociology*, vol. 44, pp. 1–24.

Wolff, E. (1966), *Peasants* (Englewood Cliffs: Prentice Hall).

Wolff, P. (1950), *The Sociology of Georg Simmel* (Glencoe: Free Press).

Wrigley, E. A. (1967), 'A simple model of London's importance in changing English society and economy 1650–1750', *Past and Present*, vol. 37, pp. 44–70.

Wünder, H. (1978, 'Peasant organisation and class conflict in East and West Germany', *Past and Present*, no. 78, pp. 47–55.

Zagorin, P. (1969), *The Court and the Gentry* (London: Routledge & Kegan Paul).

Index